# ABOUT THE AUTHOR

Sarah Foot lives at St Mellion, near Callington, with her husband and two children. Formerly on the staff of the *London Evening News,* she contributes regularly to *The Western Morning News.*

This is Sarah Foot's third title for Bossiney. In 1979 she wrote *Following the River Fowey,* a personal portrait of the lovely Fowey from its beginnings on Bodmin Moor down to the sea. Then earlier in 1980 she completed *Following the Tamar,* an even longer journey in words and pictures. Both books were extremely well received, and she is currently at work on *The Cornish Countryside,* scheduled to appear in 1981.

She is the granddaughter of that great Westcountry Liberal and Methodist Isaac Foot. So this is a fascinating family portrait: granddaughter writing about her famous grandfather — and inevitably giving us an insight into the Foot family life.

The most celebrated family in the whole Westcountry, the sons of Isaac Foot have won national and international fame — and are still making news. Sarah's father is Lord Caradon, the former Sir Hugh Foot, who has enjoyed a long and distinguished career in the Colonial Service and at the United Nations. He is especially proud of helping to engineer 'the transition from Colonies to new independent nations' — and remains involved with the international issues of the day. Her uncle, Michael, has emerged as one of the great radical figures of British politics; he has been Minister for Industry and Leader of the House of Commons, as well as being a journalist and author. Her uncle, John, in 1967 became Baron Foot of Buckland Monachorum; he is the senior partner in the solicitors firm of Foot and Bowden, created by his father Isaac Foot. He has, among other things, been a great campaigner for Dartmoor and the Liberal Party, and was Chairman of the Immigrant Advisory Service. While her uncle, Sir Dingle Foot, the eldest of the sons, was

3

**The Author with her daughter, Camilla.**

Solicitor General for the Labour Government from 1964-67, and won international reputation for his passionate advocacy of all underdogs and underprivileged, particularly peoples of British colonial territories. He was also Chairman of the *Observer* Trust.

These are only some of the valuable contributions made by the family. Here in a new Bossiney venture, Sarah Foot creates an affectionate portrait of her grandfather. 'This is not a biography of Isaac Foot. It is an account of my memories of my grandfather and reminiscences of others, looking back,' says Sarah Foot.

'He was born 100 years ago in 1880. But as each year goes by I find his influence invading my thoughts and beliefs more and more.

'His sons, who all inherited many of his fine qualities, have perhaps gained far wider world recognition than he ever did. Yet they have all agreed that none of them could hold a candle to him either in his self-taught knowledge, his gift for oratory, his wit, his most endearing personality or in the way he held most closely, all through his life, to his original beliefs and ideals, never considering any compromise.

'By writing this little book about my grandfather I hope I have been able to bring alive for others his stimulating and fascinating character . . . to know him was to be enriched for life.'

# My Grandfather
# ISAAC FOOT

# Sarah Foot

*BOSSINEY BOOKS*

*First published in 1980*
*by Bossiney Books*
*St Teath, Bodmin, Cornwall*
*Designed, Typeset and printed in Great Britain by*
*Penwell Ltd., Parkwood, Callington*
*Cornwall*

**Hardcover ISBN 0 906456 44 4**
**Paperback ISBN 0 906456 43 6**

## PLATE ACKNOWLEDGMENTS

Cover painting by H.L. Gates
Cover photography by Ray Bishop
Family Tree by Paul Honeywill
Pages 4, 11, 30, 33, 58, 86, 90 Alice Lennox-Boyd
Page 61 by courtesy of Peter Dryden
Page 110 Julie Hamilton
All other photographs from the family albums

# Contents

*Isaac Foot's Bookplate*

# I

# His Family

*Look unto the Rock whence ye are hewn, and to the
hole of the pit whence ye are digged.*
                    ISAIAH Chapter 51 Verse 1.

The fact that Isaac Foot was my grandfather had a lasting effect on
my life. I do not think I was properly aware of this when he was
alive although from earliest memory I drank in his sterling
qualities. He was a true crusader for those things he considered
important in life and gave himself unstintingly to the causes for
which he fought.

He was a radical, uncompromising Liberal, a staunch Methodist
of illuminating faith, an eloquent orator, a lover of life and a learned
man who taught himself everything he knew.

Born in 1880 into a large family, his father was a builder and
carpenter who came from the Devon village of Horrabridge to
Plymouth and built his own house in Notte Street with a workshop
attached. My grandfather's early childhood was spent with his six
brothers and sisters in that part of Plymouth where street fights
were common-place and drunken brawling quite frequent.

By the time I knew him he had become a highly successful lawyer,
a politician of some standing, a local preacher of great eloquence, a
collector of one of the largest private libraries in England, and the
father of five sons and two daughters all of whom inherited, to some
extent, his intellect and love of literature.

Our first meeting is not one I remember as I was only a few weeks
old and so was the Second World War. My mother took me and my
two year old brother for refuge to Pencrebar, the house just outside
Callington in Cornwall which he had made the all-encompassing
family home. My father, having witnessed my existence, had been
sent off to Amman.

This was the house that was to mean home to me all through my
childhood and until I was married. As my parents were always on

the move abroad, we never had a permanent base and so Pencrebar played the part. This was the centre, created by my grandparents, from which their varied family of seven children could go out into the world but know they could always return and be made to feel welcome.

It was a magic house with all the ingredients, it seemed to me, essential for a happy home.

To begin with it was always full of uncles and aunts who adored children and four of them, being without children of their own and so unused to everyday child rearing, were only too pleased to amuse their nephews and nieces.

There were endless games on the wide terraced lawn looking down on the wooded slopes of the Lynher valley. The favourite game we called 'French and English'. Two teams took their shoes off and placed them at either end of the long lawn, the object being to capture the other team's shoes to your end of the garden without being caught.

I can remember Uncle Michael, who enthusiastically joined in and

**Isaac Foot and his wife Eva with their sons John (Lord Foot), Mac (Lord Caradon) and their first two grandchildren, Kate and Paul.**

**Isaac and Eva on the lawn at Pencrebar with four grandchildren, the Author holding his right hand.**

organised endless games, throwing himself down on the garden steps trying to recover his breath and wheezing quite frightfully from his asthma as he laughed helplessly at us all.

There was Uncle Chris who always came with brown paper parcels of sweets and fruit, who saw us off on trains always with a comic and an apple, who fetched and carried for one and all, surely the most unselfish man I have ever known.

Uncle Johnnie, who lived with his wife, Anne, and children, Kate and Winslow, at nearby Crapstone, was often there. We went frequently to their house for some of the holidays and at Christmas the special treat was Uncle Johnnie's puppet show in the little theatre he built himself. He was the only one of the uncles who inherited his grandfather's gift of being clever with his hands as well as his mind and was always busy constructing something in his workshop.

Uncle Dingle, the eldest uncle, was more sedate, slightly aloof and

9

yet the first one ready for a practical joke and as we learned later a great sender of seaside postcards of slightly dubious humour. He could take a joke against himself as well as he could think up those to play against others. It was to him we always gave the glass that had a small hole half way down which meant that as the victim drank a drip dribbled down his chin. It made us children laugh until we cried. I never discovered whether Uncle Dingle really was so absent minded that he forgot the glass from one visit to another, as he surreptitiously wiped his chin looking slightly embarrassed, or whether he knew it gave us so much pleasure that he gallantly fell for the joke every time.

Either way the coming home of an uncle was always an excitement of a quite intoxicating kind.

For some time, when I used to stay at Pencrebar after my grand-mother's death in 1946, both my aunts were in residence. Aunt Jennifer ran the domestic side of life having returned from India with her husband and her two eldest children.

With her hair twisted on top of her head, with her warm smile, gentle ways and fine features; with her sturdy frame and her deep chuckle of a laugh; with her obvious concern and compassion for all the family's problems, she eventually took the place of my grand-mother in the family. She bore everyone's woes and complaints as if they were her own, becoming irate when anyone criticized any member of the family unfairly. I learned to love her well at an early age and have remained devoted to her ever after.

She was as intelligent and well read as her five clever brothers. Part of her education took place in France where she learned to speak the language fluently and to love French literature. Recently she told me how impressed she had been to find her father teaching himself French at a fairly advanced age so that he could read the French classics in the original, his markings in his French books being written in that language.

Aunt Jennifer reigned supreme in the kitchen where the huge scrubbed pine table stood and the Esse stove warmed the large pans of milk for cream and the pictures from the Hiawatha story hung on the wall. I could sit there for hours and feel the contentment and warmth that Aunt Jennifer seemed to instil into the room. In those days it was in the kitchen that we ate most meals, where we enjoyed the gaiety of family gatherings at lunch or dinner. The dining room was kept for special occasions.

Through the wide sashed windows of the kitchen, I could look across the courtyard to the stables, and for some years my Aunt Sally filled this lovely building with her ponies and horses and ran a small private riding school. The tennis court was sanded over and used as the riding school where this unrelenting tutor coached us for hours hardly ever giving praise. My cousin Kate and I were the horse lovers of our generation and we worshipped this aunt, admiring her for her skill and devotion to her horses and for the perfection she demanded from anyone working in her stables or riding her horses. She too was steeped in literature and particularly poetry which she would often recite to us as we rode through the country lanes.

When we were a bit older she gave us ponies of our own. I can still remember taking my pony, a Dartmoor called Mulberry, from the stables the first day that she was mine, and letting her out in the field. Standing by the little iron gate opposite the front door I watched her cantering away down the hill. This, I thought, must be the most perfect moment of my life. I knew the instance would be

**The kitchen window at Pencrebar: 'I could look across the courtyard to the stables . . . '**

frozen bright and clear in my memory forever — it seemed I had never before known such supreme happiness.

Through the aunts' and uncles' attentions and just their presence the strong family ties were made never to be broken.

At the head of it all was my grandfather. It was impossible not to treat him with respect although it was something he did not need to demand. His affection to us was all-embracing, making allowances where shortcomings occurred but glorying in our triumphs or virtues and finding them where others might have missed them.

Often he would stop me as I rushed past him in the dark hall at the foot of the stairs. 'And who is this?' he would joke. 'What is your name?' 'Sarah,' I would answer, breathless and in a hurry on some urgent mission. 'Sarah,' he would repeat, 'I don't think I know a Sarah. Have you no other name?' 'Sarah Dingle Foot,' I would exclaim and laughing he would send me on my way saying, 'Ah! my granddaughter Sarah Dingle.'

He was proud of our names and had taken part in the choosing of

**The Author and her cousin, Kate, at Pencrebar: 'When we were a bit older she gave us ponies of our own . . .'**

**Tea on the lawn at Pencrebar: Isaac with his second wife, Kitty, his son, Michael, and granddaughter, Alison.**

them and liked to hear us recite them in full.

My elder brother was called Paul, after one of my grandfather's heroes St Paul, and Mackintosh, my grandmother's maiden name. My second brother was called Oliver, after my grandfather's other great hero Oliver Cromwell, and Isaac which had not only been my grandfather's name but that of his father before him. My youngest brother was called Benjamin Arthur. Benjamin he approved of but he telegrammed my mother in Nigeria where my brother was born and asked, 'Who is this Arthur?' Arthur was in fact the name of my maternal grandfather and on remembering this he sanctioned the christening which took place some months later in the drawing room of Pencrebar on my parents return from Africa. My name, Sarah Dingle, was that of my Cornish great grandmother who came from Callington.

How my grandfather would make us laugh. When we were still quite small he would always come to say goodnight to us when we were tucked up in our beds. His favourite game would start as he approached the corridor to our rooms from the top of the stairs.

With one arm pulled up into his sleeve and his face in a ghastly grimace he would recite in a terrifying voice, 'Tonight we have two babes to slaughter, shall it be done my Lord? I think it oughta!' Or on other occasions he would growl, 'Fee Fi Fo Fum, I smell the blood of an Englishman, Be he alive or be he dead, I'll grind his bones to make my bread!' At which he would enter the room and throw himself on one of our beds, roaring with laughter.

How we screamed with delight, how we buried under the bedclothes half with terror half with joy. How the aunts and mothers admonished him for over-exciting the children and how he and we enjoyed it all.

I think he was the happiest man I have ever known. He must have been cross, he certainly suffered great disappointments — the death of his wife, his defeat seven times in elections are just some examples. He must have had irritations and aggravations but I honestly never remember seeing him other than full of enthusiasm. Rages he vented, certainly, over an unjust world and the consequences on others but he obviously considered himself a most fortunate man and the happiness he felt he passed so easily to others.

Meal times were always a treat for amongst the political talk and the general discussions on current affairs and literary interests my grandfather would delight us with his galaxy of funny stories. Most of them were told of Westcountry people and his already marked Westcountry speech thickened as he warmed to his subject. Often the stories made fun of the subjects he in fact took most seriously, religion, politics, literature, the law.

One of his favourite stories was about two Westcountry farmers who attended their Methodist service as usual one Sunday. The sermon consisted of a long discourse on the ten commandments and a harangue from the preacher to the congregation on the importance of obeying the commandments. When the service was over the farmers left the chapel and walked the few miles home in heavy silence and apparently deep in thought. On reaching their home they sat still obviously taken up with contemplation of the subject of the fiery sermon. Finally the silence was broken by one saying thoughtfully, 'Well! in any case, we haven't worshipped any graven images lately.' Quite often nowadays when I am feeling dissatisfied with my general performance, or when things seem to be going very

14

wrong, I mutter those words to myself, 'Well, in any case, I haven't worshipped any graven images lately,' and it never fails to make me laugh.

He took great delight in getting his grandchildren to learn pieces of his favourite poetry — often paying them small sums of money to encourage them. But we were not the only ones he taught to memorize prose and poetry. When he was Lord Mayor of Plymouth he taught his chauffeur, Fred Jarvis, who would drive him back to Callington after official functions, the whole of Gray's *Elegy Written in a Churchyard*, so that the hours spent in the car were never, in his view, wasted. When I spoke to Mr Jarvis recently he told me, 'I never really liked poetry and didn't have much of an education but when you heard Mr Foot recite poems it was the most beautiful thing in the world!'

Only once did I stay at Pencrebar, when I was old enough to remember, while my grandmother was still alive, and one of the

**The family at Pencrebar in the 1930s. From left. Back row: Christopher, Michael, Hugh (Mac), Dingle, John. Front row: Sylvia (Hugh's wife), Anne (John's wife), Isaac, Eva, their daughter Sally and Dorothy (Dingle's wife).**

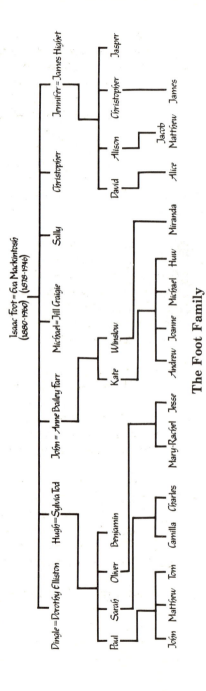

The Foot Family

saddest losses I feel is that I never knew her better. At that time and many years after there were lots of Irish setters at Pencrebar and my grandfather adored them. The eldest of the tribe was Roddy, his favourite, and later there was Johnnie who took his place in the popularity poll. There was Joe who belonged to my Uncle John and Jessica who came from a little mixed breeding and was shiny black and my favourite in spite of the fact that not long after the war she once ate the entire contents of my sweet ration. I can still see her wandering around the bedroom trying to dislodge a Mars bar from her mouth. I remember my grandmother gently introducing me to these dogs when I was only about five years old, persuading me not to be afraid of them when they played in a rowdy manner.

Over and over again all through my life people have told me how wonderful my grandmother, Eva Foot, was. It was from her side of the family I inherited my Cornish blood, of which I am so proud, and my name. My grandfather was a Devon man, who later lost his heart to Cornwall. And it was because of her wish that I was christened in the Sunday School room of the Methodist Chapel in Callington which she had just been responsible for re-roofing and re-flooring.

'Quietly she was a great help to so many people around Callington,' Olive Venning an old friend of the family told me. 'She never made a fuss about it and not many people knew of all the things she did for so many.' Mrs Venning had known my grandmother from her youth when she had been in her Sunday school class and later attended the wedding of my grandparents in Callington.

Canon Martin Andrews, now ninety-four years old, and one of the most loved and famous characters of Cornwall, told me, 'She was the greatest of all the Foot family and I was always very fond of her, and she was very kind to me.' George Roseveare, now retired, once a butcher of Callington where his father had been butcher before, a Liberal and Methodist, told me, 'If ever there was a saint it was Eva Foot.'

And certainly she was loved and respected by all her children who still speak of her with a kind of reverence. Although I was small and sick at the time when she died and we were living in Jamaica, I will never forget seeing my father when he had just been told of her death. I had not been told the news because I was ill but, when he

17

came into my room to visit me having been told only a short time before of the tragedy, I knew that some terrible, irretrievable sadness had happened. I have never again seen a man's face so broken with grief.

Eva Foot, née Mackintosh, daughter of a Scottish doctor, had been looking after her maternal grandfather, Mr William Dingle, nicknamed Gruffy, who lived in Callington, when she met Isaac at a Methodist convention. Some of the older inhabitants of the town can remember my grandfather coming to call on her. 'He wore a tall silk hat and a frock coat, which was not something we saw everyday here.' I was told.

Recently my Aunt Jennifer lent me the little leather diary my grandfather kept during the year 1901, the year he met my grandmother, proposed to her and was accepted. It is a touching account of his courtship. On 11 May 1901, a Saturday, the entry reads:

*Callington 11.5 train. Called at office before leaving. Rode to Herbert's for music. Splendid ride down by coach. Mr D. (Dingle, my grandmother's grandfather with whom she was living in Callington) met me. Dinner: rode to Kit Hill and walked. Eva said 'Yes'. Glorious time on hill top. Tea: walk to Frogwell. Spoke to Mr D. Result favourable. This day a red letter day in my history. 'Praise God from whom all blessings flow.'*

Only six weeks before it appears he had met my grandmother on a Wesleyan outing to Cambridge and had since then taken every opportunity to travel to Callington to see or meet her and when she came to Plymouth they would walk on the Hoe and lunch at Goodbody's. Though the courtship was to be so short and heady the engagement was to last a long time, presumably while my grandfather was settling into his legal practice.

They were married three years later in 1904 in West End Methodist Chapel, Callington. 'I can remember their wedding well,' Mrs Venning told me. 'We thought it was a very grand affair. The Blight sisters were their bridesmaids and they went to Switzerland for their honeymoon.'

He was only twenty one the year they became engaged, my grandmother was two years older, but the love affair lasted until she died.

Forty years after the year of their engagement my grandfather

**Isaac and Eva were married in 1904 at West End Methodist Chapel, Callington in Cornwall.**

went to America on a lecture tour during the Second World War and my grandmother wrote to him on his departure:

> *I came home today feeling sad; I don't like the idea of you being away so long and all the risks you run, it would have been so much easier for me if I could have gone with you; but that of course was impossible.*
>
> *I shouldn't feel like this when I have been wanting you to have the opportunity to go for so long; I feel it is your job. You know my special gift for saying the wrong thing at the wrong time in the wrong way but I have a heart and it all goes with you; the children only come a close second.*
>
> *All love and good wishes*
> *Eva*

On their fortieth wedding anniversary Isaac sent a little note with the present he gave her and he ended with a quotation, 'No Spring, nor Summer Beauty hath such grace as I have seen in one Autumnal face.' A few years later when she died he used these same words on the Hymn sheet for her Memorial Service.

She was the perfect partner in life for my grandfather. Equalling him in intelligence she had a more practical outlook and a very strong character and devoted herself to his welfare and that of the children though continuing with her own interests and work.

She had an eye for beautiful things, bought paintings and pieces of furniture with care and was not at all inclined to the garish or plushness of new and modern equipment or decorations. So the drawing room at Pencrebar was in soft faded chintzes — the dining room hung with early nineteenth century Cornish paintings, the furniture chosen for its beauty and its practicality always perfectly right for each room. There was a feeling of comfort everywhere without luxury.

She was the one to discipline the seven children and obedience to her wishes was absolute. She was also the one to make sure my grandfather appeared on time for functions and properly dressed, as he was famously absent minded. She accompanied him during all his political campaigns and spoke for him in his constituency joining in the canvassing with enthusiasm and determination.

She enjoyed travelling with him abroad. During the 1930s they visited Europe on several occasions, seeing Venice and Rome and Vienna, but her real love remained the little market town of Callington.

Lord Birkett, the former Justice of Appeal and one time Liberal Member of Parliament for Nottingham and a close friend of Isaac's, wrote in *The Times* at the time of my grandfather's death:

' . . . Isaac Foot among his sons and daughters was the most remarkable of them all. His pride in his family was naturally very great but the pride of the family for him was even greater. He had made himself a man of great culture and learning. His house was filled to overflowing with books and their virtue had somehow gone into him. He it was who set the pattern of public life and was the guide, counsellor and beloved leader of his notable family. Differences of view and outlook were bound to arise but the wise understanding, tolerant attitude of the father and the affectionate admiration of the family never allowed the family relationship to be

20

Below: Isaac and Eva's seven children. Left: Dingle, John and Mac.

affected.

'This atmosphere of the home was very dear to the father and was, I am certain, the best possible training ground for public life.'

When talking about his family my grandfather once recorded the story of the drummer from Horrabridge. 'A very small man with a very big drum. Performing his drum one day and beating it with great vigour he lost sight of the fact that the band in front had gone on a road to the right and he continued 100 yards on his own. A little boy overtook him and said, "Look here mister, band's gone that way." "That's all right son. Don't you trouble about that, we're playing the same tune all right." Well I think that the same tune is being played by the family all right and I am rather gratified at the tune.' He added, 'Before I was married I had seven theories as to the way to bring up children and now I have seven children and no theories at all.'

There was a sort of tribal feeling in the family circle. Everyone always ready to ridicule and criticise each other but heaven help anyone outside the family trying to do the same. My grandfather would say 'If anyone bites the Foot family they bite granite.' Because there were so many children they did not feel the need for close friends outside the family circle. And now though they remain ultra critical between themselves their loyalty to one another is absolute. Some words of his about family relationships have always stuck in my mind: 'You don't count things against your brother. A man who reckoned things against his brother would be like a man who took a promissory note from his wife or asked his mother for an IOU.'

One of the things the family liked to do together was to attend Plymouth Argyle football matches and all the family remained loyal to the team ever afterwards. My grandfather enjoyed every minute of these occasions and would shout and cheer louder than anyone else in the entire crowd at the Home Park Football Ground in Plymouth, often embarrassing us when we were younger. When Plymouth Argyle was defeated there was a general air of gloom around the house and just as much rejoicing when they won. We were initiated into this tribal custom of support for Plymouth

**Isaac and his sons at a
Plymouth Argyle football match▶**

Argyle at a very early age and the same loyalty has now travelled to a third generation as my brothers' sons and mine attend every Plymouth Argyle match they can possibly make, even when it means travelling half way across England.

All his life my grandfather took a keen interest in sport, particularly cricket and football. In 1928 he presented the Isaac Foot cup to the Callington Cricket Club and it is still the prize for one of the keenest competitions in the area. One of his most enjoyable recreations was to umpire the matches on the green field above Callington.

During the summer he would demand to know at frequent intervals what the Test Match score was and he knew all the names and attributes of the players. In the 1950s he wrote the following letter which was published in *The Times* about a Callington match:

*Sir, Two years ago when England recovered the Ashes you generously allowed me to recall the game at the Oval in 1902, when Gilbert Jessop enabled England to win by one wicket. Last evening I saw another match quite as exciting and even more glorious.*

*It was the last match of the knock-out competition between about 20 village teams which has been played for many years on our cricket ground here at Callington. Over 30 matches have been played and this was the final with some 600 of us snatching this brief interval of calm after the terrific storm of the day before.*

*Under our rules 20 overs are allowed to each side. The batsmen from Werrington (a small neighbouring parish) had scored 50 runs. Their opponents, St Dominick, batting first had scored 53. Five Werrington wickets had fallen: there was still five left to fall but (under our rules) this was the last over. The first ball was hit but did not count as the wicket was shattered. The next batsman came in, and he also hit the ball, but was run out. In came the next man, and he too, having hit the ball could not get home in time. Three balls, three wickets, three hits, but no runs!*

*The next two balls yielded three runs, but in this effort, another batsman (tempted by an over-throw) was run out. That made the score level at 53. Then came the last man to take the ball. Our hearts bled for him as he made his way down the field, Werrington's last man and last hope. Running forward he hit the ball about mid-wicket. Here again the bails were struck off, but not in time. Both men were home by less than a split second: their bodies prone, their bats outstretched.*

*In your sports page today we read about the great doings of the mighty men elsewhere. Can you find room, Sir, for this story of younger but not lesser men? Cricket is a great leveller.*

*I am, Sir, your obedient servant,*
*Isaac Foot*

*Pencrebar, Callington, Cornwall. July 31.*

Another family event I used to look forward to with great anticipation was going to the pantomine in Plymouth at Christmas time. I can remember waiting with mounting excitement as the great day approached, fearful that something would happen to cancel the event. It was always fun to go with the uncles, they spoilt us greatly, buying the inevitable box of chocolates, booking the best seats and then joining in the performance calling out eagerly the answers expected from a lively audience at a pantomime. Their enthusiasm and joy in simple pleasures was always a delight to us children.

If there was a family motto it was 'Pit and Rock'. The phrase with which the family often signed telegrams and letters to each other. When my father and uncles had been sent off to school my grandfather admonished them with a quotation from Isaiah to remember the pit whence they were dug and the rock whence they were hewn. So the phrase 'Pit and Rock' became a sort of greeting and reminder of the family traditions, and one that was often sent to comfort or sustain those who were facing difficulties.

This same phrase would be used on our birthday telegrams which arrived from my grandfather wherever we were in the world. I never felt the day to be complete without the arrival of the missive.

My grandfather was enormously generous, not only to his own family but to many people, some whom he hardly knew, who wrote to him for financial help. My mother always tells me how he used to laugh when my father who was in the habit of borrowing his father's car frequently had minor or major car crashes. 'You chump,' he would say, chuckling away. 'How did you manage it?' My father once told me the story of how my grandfather offered to pay off all his debts before he got married. My father not daring to declare exactly how much he owed only admitted to half the actual sum, but my grandfather gave him double the amount anyway.

He loved to tease us children and would often offer us either 2s 6d or half a crown when we were too young to realise it was the same amount. He would laugh to see us puzzling which to choose as we hoped that we would select the greater prize. All his children inherited this amazing generosity, and will give unstintingly even when they cannot afford it, not only financially but with their time and attentions, especially to members of the family.

Growing up amidst this warmth of giving, loving and protecting left a profound mark on me so that the one fault I cannot abide in other people now is that of meanness in thought, word or deed.

**The view from Ramsland at St Cleer, the family home on the edge of Bodmin Moor.**

# II

# His House

*I have loved the habitation of thy house: and the place whence thine honour dwelleth.*
*PSALM XXII Verse 8.*

It is often thought that the main reason my grandfather moved from his house in Lipson Terrace, Plymouth, to Pencrebar near Callington was that he ran out of room for his books in the terraced house in his beloved city of Plymouth and needed more space to house his library. But it was not only books but the growing of his children which also forced a move.

The family lived for a time during the First World War in a house on the edge of Bodmin Moor at St Cleer where two of the children were born and it is this house of which my uncles and aunts have many fond memories. My father remembers making friends with the gypsies on the moor and my Aunt Jennifer still thinks of that part of Cornwall as her home, as she was born there.

My grandmother would often walk down to the banks of the Fowey River at Redgate, especially in the spring when the bluebells in the woods there were so plentiful and beautiful.

They had a donkey to pull their 'jingle' and my grandfather made the daily journey into Plymouth and his solicitor's office from Liskeard station to which he either walked or rode each day, my grandmother often driving the jingle in to meet him in the evenings. This donkey was to cause some trouble as he was always escaping from his field. Eventually a letter for Isaac arrived from the Local Authority saying that protests had been made about the depredations of this donkey upon neighbouring property.

My grandfather replied that 'for myself, I am powerless to control the animal, but I have read your letter to the donkey . . .'

The pretty little Georgian house must have bulged at the seams when all the children were there but they all talk of it with fond remembrance. When my father was made a life peer it was from this area he took his new name, Lord Caradon — from the moorland hill nearby — of St Cleer, the small town at the end of the bumpy lane which led to their house. At the beginning of this moorland lane is a large chunk of granite with a plaque stating my grandfather's name and the date of his birth and death, placed there after his death in remembrance of his time spent at St Cleer.

It was during the years when they lived here that the family acquired their long lasting love of Bodmin Moor and since they walked all over its boggy and hilly lands they knew it well and my father still talks of Caradon Hill and Brown Willy as his favourite places in the world.

But it had been one of my grandmother's earliest wishes that she might one day live in Pencrebar. Callington had been her mother's home and she remained faithful to the town all her life. It was through one of his life long friends Mr Arthur Blight, a member of the famous family of solicitors of Callington, that my grandfather came to buy Pencrebar. Mr Blight had informed him that the property was on the market and one evening he went to see it. As he drove up the drive the house and garden were bathed in a dramatic sunset and his heart was lost to the place instantly. He returned to see Mr Blight and said, 'You've sold me a sunset', and Pencrebar was soon his.

So in 1927 they moved to the white Victorian manor house just outside Callington with its three peaked facade, wide sashed windows, large rooms and out-houses and wide sweeping lawns and shrubberies. It became a home for the family and a symbol to many of the local people of Liberalism, Methodism and of course literature. It was here that they so often gathered to discuss these interests and to celebrate or commiserate.

All through my life the returning to Pencrebar was an exciting and comforting event. When I was at prep school in Dorset and my parents were abroad in Nigeria some of each holiday was spent there. Sometimes my grandfather would come and meet us at Tavistock Station when we arrived from London. He was a notoriously bad driver, though he could never see this fault in himself. He would always, without fail, back the car until it hit something and when we children all screamed at him to be more cautious he would say, 'What do you think bumpers are for?' This practice of backing until you hit something was pretty lethal at

28

Ramsland where the family lived in the First World War.

Tavistock Station as the parking lot was on a high and precipitous hill and I was always afraid we would go over the edge.

As we drove towards Pencrebar the excitement would mount. Crossing the bridge at Gunnislake he would make us spell out, D-E-V-O-N and then C-O-R-N-W-A-L-L and on the last letter we would shout out with joy. We had crossed the Tamar River and were back home in Cornwall.

In the library the fire would be burning, in the kitchen were delicious things to eat, pasties, clotted cream and junket, freshly baked bread. In our bedrooms were thick eiderdowns and hot water bottles and the familiar smell of old books, furniture polish and wood smoke. My cousin Kate and I were sometimes lent my Aunt Sally's wireless so we could lie in bed and listen to programmes like *Much Binding in the Marsh*, over which we wept with laughter, and *Dick Barton, Special Agent*.

Sometimes, on the first morning of the holidays, I would wake up and before I was properly conscious feel the faint dread of another

**Pencrebar at Callington: 'As we drove towards Pencrebar the excitement would mount . . .'**

school day. Then I would hear the rooks cawing in the copse opposite the front door, and that sound would make my semi-conscious mind register — I was back at home. The feeling of content and happiness I can still resurrect now and I am often reminded of it when I hear the sound of rooks calling to one another.

I suppose the reason these childhood memories remain so bright and clear cut is because, at that time of life, there is nothing to worry or distract the mind.

I can still smell the wonderful heady scent of newly mown grass as Kate and I would lie flat on the lawn at Pencrebar soaking in the first real sunshine of the year, talking or just thinking. A wonderful languorous feeling as the sun seemed to get right through to the bones, the first promise of hot summer days to come.

On the opposite side of the wide sweeping drive to the front door was a swing. I could spend hours and hours on that swing; if you went really high you could see right over the woods and down the valley. It was always a ritual for me that the last thing I would do before leaving Pencrebar was to go on the swing. It was a comforting way of saying goodbye, a way of gearing one's mind to meet new situations.

I was obviously worried at one point after my grandmother's death that my grandfather was nurturing thoughts of leaving this lovely house as the aunts had left to find other occupations. I was nine years old when I wrote the following schoolgirl letter found amongst his papers after his death:

*Dear Grandpa,*

*I hope you are well. How are all the ponies? I am in bed with mumps. Is Auntie Jen with you or not, where is she if she isn't with you? Are you living by yourself or not? I have written five letters already today.*

*Matron says the pain of the mumps will go away today and the swelling will go down in a week.*

*How is Roddy and Johnny?* (his dogs) *Thank you very much for letting me stay last hols at Pencrebar. I enjoyed it very much. Do stay at Pencrebar.*

*Love from*
*Sarah Dingle Foot*

*P.S. Please write soon.*

*(Sketch of me with mumps)*

He stayed and when he was seventy married again. My uncles and aunts found it hard to accept a new mistress of the house — a step-mother. Their mother had been such a remarkable woman there was none who could take her place. But Kitty, his second wife, was wonderfully warm-hearted, looked after my grandfather magnificently, gave him the worship and adoration and the comfort that he well deserved these last ten years of his life. She too fell in love with Pencrebar and made the grandchildren feel very welcome to come there whenever they liked.

So when I was working in London I went with groups of friends whenever I could. I always wanted my friends to meet my grandfather, to be at Pencrebar, to feel the magic.

Each time I returned all the old haunts had to be visited. Down to the Lynher River we went, over Newbridge to walk along the river banks and then from one little island to another and paddle near the rapids. It was here that we used to sail paper boats made from old voting posters found in the attic at Pencrebar. Vote for Isaac Foot, Dingle Foot, John Foot they read, and we watched them snaking their way down the bright, clear, dappled water of that beautifully wooded river. Then we would do the stiff walk to the top of bracken covered Cadson Bury, an Iron Age fort, and sit at the top puffing heavily, and gaze down at the sparkling Lynher below. This was all my grandfather's land and how he loved it.

Other days we would walk through Pencrebar woods to the Witch's Hut, a little house with one room and a verandah where I thought it would be lovely to live forever. In the spring the bluebells were thick on the ground giving a mauve haze to the surrounding land. My grandfather in younger days sometimes went to this hut in the woods to write and read in the peace and quiet it offered.

On bright clear days my grandfather would say, 'You must take your friends to Kit Hill'. He always maintained it afforded the finest view in the Kingdom! Once before the reign of Henry III it had been the meeting place of the old Cornish and Devon Parliament of Tinners, and meetings in commemoration of this are still held there. Here we would wander looking down at the gaunt and seemingly bottomless pool of the old quarry. Tin and granite were once mined here in abundance. Then up on the moorland crest of this hill to look

**Lynher River: ' . . . we paddled near the rapids.'▶**

**Isaac by the Lynher with his dog, Roddy.**

down on what seemed like the whole of Devon and Cornwall. He was right, it is one of the greatest views ever to be seen.

By the time my grandfather married for the second time there were fewer people coming and going in the great house. No more ponies in the stables, the tennis court was covered with weeds, Mr Worth, the beloved gardener, had left and the vegetable garden no longer brought forth fruit and vegetables in abundance.

I could remember the days when we had gone to talk to Mr Worth up in the huge vegetable garden. I had loved the sound of his deep Cornish voice and it was a magic place in Spring when the borders to all the beds were thick with sweet smelling lily of the valley.

Once, in later years, when travelling down to Pencrebar with a group of friends, our car broke down when we were crossing Dartmoor and we spent several hours just outside Ashburton trying to get the old car going. Eventually we arrived at Pencrebar at four o'clock in the morning. We tiptoed up the backstairs, found electric blankets on and sheets turned back and we crept into bed exhausted but happy to be home.

A few hours later I woke to find my grandfather putting a rather slopped-in-the-saucer cup of tea on my bedside table. It was always his habit to wake very early and to take cups of tea to those of the family staying. It never occurred to him that 6 a.m. was not a time everyone needed sustenance — that some of us after a week's hard play and hard work in London longed to sleep on until later.

That morning he sat on the end of my bed and enquired about our journey. Why? he wondered, had we gone via Ashburton. Quite the wrong route. 'Ashburton, Ashburton', he repeated incredulously rolling his r's in his lovely Westcountry voice. But what worried him most was that the electric light over the backdoor had been left on for our benefit all night. This most generous man who gave so magnanimously to so many all his life could never bear to see the wastage of electricity.

He would often roam the house turning off lights and grumbling as he went. It was a positive fetish with him. And I suppose since the luxury of electricity had come about during his lifetime it was understandable that he would treat it with care and thrift.

Things had certainly changed since my grandparents first moved into Pencrebar in 1927.

Ruth Stephens who lives in Callington was able to tell me about those early days. At fourteen years of age she had gone to Pencrebar as a parlour maid a few months after my grandparents moved in and had lived in the house until she was married seven years later.

Speaking of my grandmother she said, 'She was like a second mother to me all those years and I was made to feel one of the family.' The day began for Ruth in those days, 'With a knock on the door at 6 a.m. and Mrs Foot would leave us a pot of tea; I shared a room with the cook.' At six-thirty they were downstairs and laying the breakfast and preparing it.

'At eight o'clock sharp the gong went for breakfast and everyone was expected to be there on time. Straight after breakfast the whole household gathered for morning prayers in the dining room. Then Mr Foot would leave for his solicitor's office in Plymouth. Every morning Mrs Foot and I waited at the window of the dining room for you could be sure that Mr Foot would have forgotten something. Half way down the drive he would toot his horn, shout what he needed, and I would rush across the lawn to take him whatever he had left.' She laughs at the memory.

'After my days off I would catch a bus back to Pencrebar and one of the boys was always sent to meet me at the gate and walk with me up the drive. Then I got a boy-friend and I didn't know how to get rid of them!

'Mrs Foot always had a rest in the afternoons and she insisted I did too. "You get right into bed Ruth," she would say, "and have a proper rest."

'Then we would often sit in the big bay window of her bedroom and do the sewing and mending. When all the boys were away at school or university there were so many name tapes to sew on and Mrs Foot never wasted anything. All the clothes and linen were carefully mended. She also made all the jam and marmalade and did a lot of the baking and laundered most of the clothes.

'The first time I ever went to Plymouth was when Mr and Mrs Foot took me. Mr Foot went to the office and Mrs Foot took me to the tea rooms and we had cakes and a cup of tea. I thought it was the most exciting thing that had ever happened to me.

'Then I remember Mr Foot took a box at the old Royal Theatre in Plymouth and he took all the family and myself to see *The Gondoliers*. I can remember every minute of it now so clearly.

'When Mr Foot went electioneering I often went, too, to keep Jennifer company. It was very exciting.'

My grandfather was given a grand piano by the Totnes Division after he lost the election of 1910 but having greatly increased the Liberal vote. The plaque on the piano reads:

> *Presented to Isaac Foot*
> *By the Liberals of Totnes Division*
> *In recognition of his strenuous fight*
> *Made by him at the General Election 1910.*

The piano was one of his proudest possessions and he loved to play.

Ruth Stephens remembers, 'He always played hymns on Sundays and sang loudly. His favourite was *Beulah Land*, which had been his father's favourite hymn too.' This was a habit he kept up all through my childhood. I can still hear his voice as he sung out the words,

> *O Beulah Land, sweet Beulah Land,*
> *As on thy highest mount I stand,*
> *I look away across the sea*
> *Where mansions are prepared for me,*
> *And view the shining glory shore*
> *My heaven, my home for ever more.*

Many dignitaries came to stay at Pencrebar in those days when my grandfather was fighting elections. And Ruth remembers, 'Often they were speaking for Mr Foot at election time. I remember Sir Donald McLean, Lord Samuel, Lord Grey, Sir Norman Birkett, who came to defend Annie Hearne in the poisoning case. Mr Foot used to get them to plant trees in remembrance of their visit. Of course no drink was ever served in the house. People knew that this was Mr Foot's way and just accepted it.

'When people were staying in those days before there was running hot water we had to take all the hot water upstairs to the rooms in big jugs with basins. On one occasion when I had to take the hot water to Lord Grey's room I was told to knock and say, "It's your hot water, My Lord."

'We were giggling about this in the kitchen beforehand and the cook said I should say, "It's the Lord outside with the water." I did this and Lord Grey said, "Come in Ruth, now sit down and tell me

**Pencrebar: ' . . . a symbol to many local people of Liberalism, Methodism and literature.'**

again." He was very charming.

'At Christmas the Callington Town Band always paid a visit to Pencrebar playing carols outside the front door and then they would all come in for a cup of tea.

'We were all expected to go to chapel on Sundays. Mr and Mrs Foot always sat in the back pew, I can see Mr Foot now sitting there with his Bible open following the sermon. Sometimes I heard him preach and it was always a great experience.'

When Ruth Stephens (née Clogg) was married to her postman husband my grandmother and Aunt Jennifer attended the wedding at St Ive and Ruth kept in touch with my grandparents until they died. She still corresponds with Jennifer, her favourite of the family, the youngest daughter, who had been at Pencrebar all the time Ruth was there. When my grandmother died Ruth was given her silver thimble and it remains one of her most treasured possessions.

My grandfather had a great love for music all his life, given birth in his earliest years when he learned to sing loud and clear the Methodist hymns he loved all his life.

In his last years Johann Sebastian Bach was his great love and often when staying at Pencrebar we would wake on a Sunday morning to hear some of this great composer's music throbbing through the floorboards of the house. My grandfather would put on his favourite record as loudly as possible on his old record player and then retire to his bedroom upstairs to listen as he read. Since he never slept late in the morning, it could mean that Bach's music was an early awakener and a shock to those who were not used to the ways of the house. As his whole family were early risers none of them found it at all extraordinary that life should begin at this early hour, and with such gusto.

My grandfather never in fact slept very well and sometimes in the very early hours of the morning could be heard shuffling through the house seeking out some book he wished to read. Olive Venning who stayed at Pencrebar often in the later years remembers being woken in the middle of the night. 'I was sleeping in the Greek Testament room', she told me, 'when I was woken and saw your grandfather climbing on a chair to get down a book he wanted.

**Pencrebar: ' . . . this was the house that was to mean home to me all through my childhood.'▶**

When he turned and saw me lying there he was overcome with embarrassment. He had obviously quite forgotten I was sleeping there. He left the room quickly, apologising profusely as he went.'

What seems strange to me is the great depth of feeling we all had for Pencrebar. The family had not lived there for generations; it was only thirty years before his death that my grandfather bought it. It had been built by the Horndon family in 1849. I suppose it was not really architecturally beautiful, though I thought it, quite simply, the loveliest house in the world.

I went back not long ago to see the house before Mr and Mrs Neate sold it. They had always been kind about letting us go back and visit the house with friends, and in fact used to say, 'We always feel that we are only custodians for the Foot family.' They were in fact the second owners since my grandfather died.

The house had changed. There were bright and new wallpapers and carpets, quite a lot of modern furniture, no more books piled high in every room. The great fireplaces had been blocked up, the huge scrubbed kitchen table was no longer there and the old cooker was replaced with micro ovens and split level grills. But as I wandered round the house, walked up the back stairs, gazed at the view I could feel and smell happiness everywhere. Somehow my grandfather's voice and laughter and knowledge and music had sunk into the bricks and mortar and seemed to waft out to greet me.

I met a man in Lostwithiel a few months ago who said to me, 'I still raise my hat everytime I pass Pencrebar gates.' I replied, 'So do I.'

# III

# His Politics

*Subtleties may deceive you; integrity never will.*
                                        CROMWELL.

Isaac Foot's Liberalism and Methodism were closely linked. People often ask me how the son of a builder with little education became so successful in so many fields.

I am sure it all started with his real and burning faith and his gift of oratory — his father too had been a most eloquent local preacher — and of course his quest for knowledge. All his life he read or declaimed poetry and prose wherever he went.

At fourteen he left school and went to London as a Boy Clerk at the Paymaster General's Department at the Admiralty and he recorded once: 'I learned to read while walking and also learned to measure distances by reading. That London walk took exactly one hour, and I found that if I began reading an essay on Macaulay as I entered the first gate in Kensington Gardens I could finish it comfortably as I turned from Green Park into Spring Gardens. I found a special route across Hyde Park and was rather proud of my discovery. Generally there was not a soul to be seen, Macaulay is all the better for being read aloud and one could freely declaim a rhetorical passage without being regarded as a lunatic.'

His sojourn in London only lasted eighteen months — the call of the Westcountry was too great. He returned to Plymouth to train for his eventual career in politics and the law.

Later in life when he had formed his own solicitor's practice of Foot and Bowden in Plymouth and he moved with his family from his hometown to St Cleer on Bodmin Moor for a few years, each day he would walk the three miles or so to Liskeard Station declaiming poetry as he went. He had by this time memorised a hundred sonnets and 'I found I could do thirty of them in an hour,' he said.

In the 1930s during the 'National Government' when he was made Parliamentary Secretary for Mines he 'found that in my luncheon walk through St James's Park to and from the Reform Club, by dividing the poem into two, I could comfortably begin and complete the reading of fifty five stanzas of Shelley's *Adonais*.

He fought hard and long in politics from 1910 to 1945 and lost seven campaigns in all, sometimes by a very close margin as in December 1910 when he lost by 41 votes to Sir Reginald Pole Carew in the South East Cornwall (Bodmin) Division. It was during this campaign that he was being barracked at a meeting by a woman with a high pitched voice at the back of the hall who kept repeating, 'Vote for Pole-Carew'. He eventually retorted 'Cock-a-doodle-doo' and brought the house down with laughter.

The feelings that ran so high during those elections of the 1920s, 1930s and 1940s have been recalled for me by several old Liberals in the Bodmin constituency.

Mr Austin Toms from Looe told me he could remember Isaac being met in Looe at the bridge after the results of the 1922 election were announced. He had won for the first time and was apparently carried shoulder high in a torch-light procession through the street to the Liberal Club, which is now the site of Barclays Bank.

One of Isaac's staunchest supporters was a Looe fisherman, who had his luggers painted in the Liberal colours. Yellow sculls and blue bulwarks, a colour they maintained for the rest of their lives.

Apparently in these days shopkeepers had to stay very neutral during the elections as if it was known they had voted either Liberal or Tory only those voting for the same side would buy goods from their shops.

It is true that many old friendships were broken over the difference of opinion in politics which came to a climax on election day. One old hill farmer from Bodmin Moor told me he had given up all interest in politics when he found two of his neighbours had fallen out over a political argument. Another woman wrote to me from Fowey and told me how when the election results were announced there people were often thrown into the river by their opponents.

Everyone apparently took a keen interest in the politics of the day and were anxious to hear both sides put their points, so that the meetings prior to elections were attended by people of every conviction and hecklers were quick to try their best to disrupt speeches. My grandfather thrived on the cut and thrust and the challenge and counted heckling opponents as an asset.

At another political meeting he was asked by someone from the audience whether his name Isaac indicated he was a Jew. 'No,' he replied, 'but I intend to be one of the chosen people.'

Stanley Goodman wrote of him in the *Dictionary of National Biography:* 'Remarkable about his Commons Career was that it was all over in 8 years but in that short time he had won and presented a national fame; one of the minor tragedies of English history between the wars was that Isaac Foot was not, except for these few years, in the Commons to shape it.'

The last election he fought and lost was at Tavistock in 1945. It was a sad day at Pencrebar for Uncle John lost at Bodmin, Uncle Dingle lost at Dundee and only Uncle Michael won at Devonport and he was on the Socialist platform.

We were staying at Pencrebar on this occasion and although I was too young to remember the effect of the results of the election on the

**Isaac Foot as MP for the SE Cornwall (Bodmin) Division speaking to his constituents outside the House of Commons.**

**Isaac with sons John and Michael — they were all fighting the 1945 election.**

household my brother Paul who was aged seven and had an early feel for the importance of politics burst into tears.

I have frequently asked people who were involved in his Liberal campaigns how my grandfather bore up under defeat. Mr David Hawken, a local Liberal and Methodist preacher, who followed his political career closely told me that he always remained cheerful, sure in himself that he had fought a clean fight and having made no compromises. Mr Hawken said, 'If he had not stood up for his temperance convictions he probably would have won more votes. Many of the brewery people felt his attitude might lead to the closing of the public houses. But he was not prepared to play down his convictions.'

I have often heard the story that when he was still a young man he saw a drunk coming out of one of the pubs in the back streets of Plymouth and strike his own mother. He never got over the experience. But whether this was the reason that he remained teetotal all his life and signed the temperance pledge early on I do not know. I think he felt strongly that so many poor families suffered from the effects of the wage earner spending a good deal of the small amounts of money they had on drink; and he felt some stand must be made against this corrupting practice. He had seen evidence of the destruction drink brought on many of the poorer homes amongst which he lived as a boy and was sickened by the damage done.

He fought Nancy Astor in the Sutton Division of Plymouth in 1919 but was defeated. She was the first woman to take her seat in the House of Commons. Though he was beaten decisively in this election he and Lady Astor formed a life time fast friendship. They both shared a great love for Plymouth and were both adamant and unflinching in their teetotalism.

Once when they were travelling up to London together by train she asked if she could see what he was reading. It was one of his many commonplace books in which he wrote his favourite passages of literature and this one was devoted to one of his favourite authors — Milton.

When the train arrived in London Nancy Astor asked if she might

**The family at Pencrebar during the 1945 election: from Isaac's left are seated Sylvia, Jennifer, John, Eva, Mac, Anne and Michael.**

**Isaac and Eva Foot
canvassing in the 1920s.**

borrow it for a few days. Reluctantly Isaac lent her the book. When a week had passed he telephoned Nancy Astor's secretary and asked her to arrange for the return of his treasured book. But after repeated enquiries it was still not returned. Isaac was distraught. If the book had been lost or mislaid it could mean the end of a lasting friendship.

Eventually Lady Astor not only returned the book but presented him with several leather bound, gilt edged copies which she had had printed especially for him. The inscription on the front in gold letters reads 'to I.F. from N.A.' On the first page is printed 'Arranged by Isaac Foot and Presented to him by Nancy Astor 1935'. He was overcome and often told the story in later years.

It was during the 1919 election against Nancy Astor in the Plymouth Sutton Division that he received a letter from his old friend Sir Arthur Quiller Couch. It began: 'I am sure it is permissible for an old friend in South East Cornwall to wish you well in the battle you are fighting always with the old sincerity of mind and the old chivalry of conduct.' And it ended: 'But if it be possible, of another thing I am sure that they will do themselves honour in selecting a man who, however provoked, ever fights clean and by gentle courage dignifies the cause of the whole people which fires his heart.'

'Q' was to remain a friend of his all his life. They shared a common interest in politics and books and though from totally different backgrounds and life styles they respected each other enormously. Foy Quiller Couch, Q's daughter, told me that as a young girl she was taken to chapel by her father to hear my grandfather preach, though as a family they were pillars of the Church of England.

Of course electioneering in the 1920s when he first entered politics was a very different affair from that of today. Political meetings were well attended and feeling ran very high at these gatherings. When the results started coming in on election day people gathered at the post offices to hear the count and word spread quickly in spite of the lack of the telephone.

When the results were announced, as they were in Liskeard for the South East Cornwall (Bodmin) Division, there was often a lot of hard feeling and people have told me stories of the opponents spitting at my grandfather as he passed through the crowd when he won, and once a woman spitting in my grandmother's face. 'She did not flinch or change her expression,' I am told.

My grandfather was tough on his opponents, some thought too tough at times, but he took the same kind of treatment against himself in good heart. His sons well recollect him being hit in the back of the neck by a rotten tomato thrown from the crowd during one election, and how they thought it 'a very fine shot indeed'.

During one famous telephone conversation to a younger candidate my grandfather is reported to have advised, 'Tell them it is a lie. Tell them it is a damned lie. Tell them it is no less a lie because it is uttered by a Tory gentleman of title.'

He was known in the Westcountry as 'Our Isaac' and people still talk of him as such though he has been dead twenty years. Some people on learning my relationship with him come and tell me how they knew 'Sir Isaac', a title which he never held but which many people gave him, reckoning he deserved it.

The honour he cherished most highly was that of Privy Councillor, conferred on him after his parliamentary career was all over in 1937. It was one he remained touchingly proud of for the rest

48

of his life.

He started fighting elections in 1910 at Totnes but it was 1922 before he won in the Bodmin Division. After the results were announced in Liskeard he returned to the town of Callington which five years later was to become his home. He was met at Newbridge straddling his beloved River Lynher and was put into a huge model aeroplane in which he was drawn to the centre of the town. The streets were lined with cheering people and those who can remember the occasion told me that Callington had never known such excitement. Isaac would often say during elections that if the people of Callington were all he had to worry about he would have no worries at all.

He was returned to the Bodmin constituency in 1923 but defeated in 1924 but returned again in 1929 where he remained until 1935. So his entire Parliamentary career only lasted eight years.

On the formation of the National Government in 1931 he was

**Liberal victory announced at Liskeard — Isaac Foot addresses the crowd.**

appointed Minister for Mines and was reappointed after the reconstitution of the Government after the General Election and served as Minister until 1932 when he resigned his position on the introduction of the proposals adopted at the Imperial Conference of Ottawa. He had fought elections on the Free Trade ticket and was not going back on his word. This act probably cost him the whole of his political future but he apparently never regretted it. Convictions were there to be stood by and many of his old Liberal colleagues believed his unflinching attitude in all matters of ideals was the most outstanding part of his many-sided character.

In a speech he made in the Old Queen's Hall in London in October 1932, a fortnight after he resigned his office as Minister of Mines in protest against the Ottawa Agreements, he said: 'Free Trade was killed by the political lynch-law, and when the Third Reading of the Import Duties Bill came along and I was allowed by the grace of the Tory backbenchers to speak for about eight minutes in that great controversy, Mr Neville Chamberlain turned to me after I had finished and after they had shouted "resign", and he said "We have had tonight the passionate and despairing cry of a man who is convinced that he has seen the last of Free Trade".

'It was not despairing, but it was passionate, and it was passionate because of the way in which Free Trade fell. It did not fall in open battle.

'This Caesar did not fall in the long campaigns of Gaul and Spain, this Caesar did not go down on the stricken fields of Thapsus and Pharsalia. This Caesar fell by the stroke of the dagger of Casca Chamberlain and the sword-thrust of Cassius Simon and Brutus Runciman . . .'

'Subtlety may deceive you: integrity never will' wrote his great hero Oliver Cromwell whom he always referred to as 'The Protector' and these lines might almost have stood as his guide in his political career.

In 1930 he was appointed a member of the Round Table Conference on India and served on the second Round Table Conference in 1931. His crusading for the rights of the people during this period earned him the title of 'The Member of Parliament for the depressed areas'. He once said in a radio broadcast, 'I gave five years to India and the problem of race was there morning, noon and night.' Many people have spoken about the invaluable work he put into these conferences and meetings and in later years he would talk of it as one of the most interesting periods of his life.

One day when I was about eight years old I was driving with my grandfather from Pencrebar to my Uncle John's house near Yelverton. I had been mulling over in my mind the world of politics and was feeling somewhat confused. 'Is the Liberal party always going to be the best party to vote for?' I asked him. 'Well I think I could just forgive you if you voted Socialist but I could never forgive you if you voted Tory,' he replied. There was a twinkle in his eye but I knew he was only half joking, and I never forgot what he said.

Of course by the time I knew him well the electioneering days were over. The campaigning songs were still sung around the house or on long car journeys.

*If you want to find our Isaac*
*We know where to look*
*We know where to look*
*We know where to look*
*If you want to find our Isaac*
*We know where to look*
*Right at the top of the Poll*
*You'll find him, you'll find him*
*Right at the top of the poll.*

In the last few months when I have been asking Westcountry people who remember his political days to recount stories of that time most of them begin with this song, often singing it right through from beginning to end. Fifty years later it still rings in their ears and obviously conjures up many happy memories. I feel sad that I missed those devastating, electrifying campaigns.

For the Tavistock campaign, my father who was home from abroad wrote the following song which we children have been singing ever since particularly as we drive across Dartmoor on our way home.

*I'm going to vote, vote*
*Vote for Isaac Foot*
*He's going to win*
*He's going to win*
*From the Plym to Darty Moor*

*You can hear the people roar*
*That we'm going to put'm in.*
*My mind's made up*
*And I can see*
*That Tavistock will Liberal be*
*And Ikey Foot's the man for me.*

One more song was given to me the other day which was obviously sung during the 1922 election when he fought Sir Frederick Poole and beat him.

*Foot's a man*
*Poole's a mouse*
*Foot's a man for Parliament House.*

No doubt there were songs sung against him and the Liberals but

**Pencrebar: Isaac and Kitty Foot listening to Gerald Whitmarsh addressing a Liberal Rally . . .**

I never heard them and can find none now.

It is the Liberal Garden parties at Pencrebar that are remembered still by so many people. Thousands came from miles around for these annual events in coaches, cars, on foot and by bicycle. Some I can remember coming by horse and cart and on tractors. The lovely grounds with their rhododendrons and azaleas and huge beech and oak trees were covered quite literally with people. 'Those parties', Mrs George Roseveare told me, 'have made the name of Pencrebar familiar to Liberals throughout the Westcountry.'

Once when my grandfather was being thanked for allowing a Liberal fete to be held at Pencrebar he replied, 'Don't thank me. Pencrebar may be a lovely place, but it is never more beautiful than when filled with shining Liberal faces,' and he meant it most sincerely.

**'It is the Liberal Garden parties at Pencrebar that are remembered still . . .' Jeremy Thorpe sits on Isaac's left.**

Cyril Billing, a most gifted blacksmith who performs both artistic and practical deeds in the name of his profession remembers going to Pencrebar for one of these garden parties. He was still a boy and having had TB in his leg had recently had the leg amputated below the knee. He was struggling along on his clumsy irons with crutches and as he told me, 'I was feeling rather blue as we walked down the back lane to the house, the crutches had made me hot and rubbed me badly under the arms. Then I saw a man with no legs at all. He had two wooden boxes and he lifted his body from one to the other slowly moving each box further forward. I was struck by two things — one that he must want to get to Pencrebar pretty badly, the other that I had no right to feel sorry for myself.'

That same day Mr Billing told me he heard my Uncle Michael make what he believes must have been his first political speech. He was about thirteen years of age and his father held him aloft to address the crowd. 'There was a lot of flaying of arms and shouting,' Mr Billing told me laughing as he recalled the scene. An insight into future performances perhaps!

When Uncle Michael as a young man became a Socialist his father tried to dissuade him but Michael recorded in a broadcast that when he explained to his father that the origin of his becoming a Socialist was that he had encouraged him to read William Hazlitt his father had said, 'Oh well! if William Hazlitt was responsible that is all right with me.'

His mother's form of forgiveness came in a very different way. When he fought his first election as a Labour candidate there was still a certain feeling that his mother far from approved. But a parcel was delivered to him on the platform of his final meeting and it enclosed a Cornish pasty baked by his mother, the eventual peace offering.

In the 1950s my grandfather supported and spoke for Stuart Roseveare when he fought the Bodmin Division for the Liberal party. Cyril Billing found himself responsible for running the loudspeaker system during the election. Mr Roseveare was defeated and the victorious Conservative candidate thanked the Labour candidate for a good fight totally ignoring the Liberal opponent;

**Isaac Foot giving the address at the annual service below Cromwell's statue outside the House of Commons**▶

thus casting aspersions on the Liberals. In a fury Isaac Foot who was standing beside Stuart Roseveare grabbed the microphone and was about to make a slanderous attack on the rejoicing Tories.

'I just disconnected the microphone and told everyone there was no way I could get them to work. I did it for Mr Foot's good. He would have done himself more harm than good,' he told me.

'Your grandfather was a strange man. When he was speaking on the platform you felt he was giving his heart away. But when you met him and sat and talked with him he was quite diffident. He would sit slumped in a chair. I can see him now, and you felt as if so many cogs were turning over in his mind. You never knew quite what he was really thinking.

'I can remember him coming to St Mellion when we were children still at school and the excitement was terrific. We all wore our blue and yellow ribbons. He sang a song for us, one of his favourites — *To be a Farmer's Boy.*

'It was because of hearing him speak about Cromwell that I became so interested in him and tried to make a map of all the places Cromwell was likely to have travelled in the Westcountry. There was no man ever like your grandfather, no man who could replace him.'

He was the founder member of the Cromwellian Association and remained its President until he died, always enjoying the annual services held by the statue of Cromwell outside the Houses of Parliament.

I met a man in my village post office during the last general election. He said to me, 'I hope you are voting Liberal, your grandfather persuaded me to do so when I was a young man and I have been doing so ever since.'

And it made me wonder what my grandfather would feel about the Liberal party today. Of course he had seen the Liberal party go through many crises, he had seen it split and divided, sometimes almost wiped out and yet remaining strong in some areas, especially the Westcountry. After he had fought and lost his last election he was made President of the Party and he toured the country inspiring Liberals for the 1950 General Election.

But some of those he had faith in and great hopes for have not met his expectations. Jeremy Thorpe and Peter Bessell both felt the warmth of his encouragement, how sad my grandfather would have been to see the recent turn of events in their lives.

56

# IV

# His Methodism

*O for a trumpet voice on all the world to call.*
*CHARLES WESLEY*

There is no doubt that the springboard of all my grandfather's other varied activities during his lifetime was his firm faith and staunch Methodism. It was something I was aware of as far back as I can remember and was to affect the rest of my life. To him Christianity was a living doctrine that gave him real happiness all his life.

From a very early age when we stayed at Pencrebar we were all expected to attend chapel on Sundays. To this day I have never been into the Church at Callington but the West End Chapel was familiar from the very beginning of my life.

I cannot, of course, remember my christening which took place in the Sunday school room of the West End Chapel when I was only a few weeks old, but I do remember family services as a small child. On Sunday mornings driving with my grandfather to chapel was always an alarming occurrence as he was such an erratic driver. We would stop on the way to give a lift to those people we met who could fit into the car.

Hatted, gloved, and in their right Sunday morning minds, there was a special feeling to that chapel congregation. The chapel was always packed and the feeling of solid, communal devoutness permeated the little building.

There were always lots of children and we sat together in the front pews. We were expected to join in the service, announcing the customary children's hymn and answering the Minister's questions during the short sermon directed at the youngsters. An early example of audience participation, and one that kept our minds on what was being said.

I would troop out with the rest of the children for the Sunday school lessons during the main sermon and watching the example

**West End Chapel, Callington: '. . . we were all expected to attend chapel on Sundays.'**

set by my grandfather we all learned to sing the hymns that he loved so dearly, loud and clear, even if we had no sense of tune.

My grandfather always sat in the back pew and I can still see him, head bent, turning the pages of his Bible, looking for the text of the sermon, which, in any case, he invariably knew by heart.

When we returned to Pencrebar for Sunday lunch he would often ask us children what we thought we had learned in our Sunday school class and as we got older and remained in chapel for the sermon he would ask us what we thought of it. So we learned to pay attention and not to let our minds drift to other things anxious that we would be able to answer his questions.

Sometimes my grandfather would preach in the chapel and later I was to hear him preach in other chapels and halls. When we were living in Nigeria he came to stay with us and preached one Sunday in the large Methodist church in Lagos. He seemed as much at home surrounded by an African congregation as he was in his home town of Callington. I never heard him give a sermon without feeling

'When we were in Nigeria, my grandfather came to stay.'

enriched by the experience. I often thought that sooner or later he would disappoint me, afraid that the eloquence and inspiration and adeptness might grow dim as he got older, but I was never let down.

His faith and the joy he derived from it was almost overpowering. But there was nothing sombre about his religious feeling. It lit up his life from within and that he was able to impart this to others was a real reward for us. Even now reading the scripts of his sermons or his broadcasts on religious subjects the strength of his living faith comes through with enormous power, so that I can remember the sound of his voice and the great brilliance with which he could impart his religious experience. In the Looe area, on Bodmin Moor, at Calstock and Saltash, I have met people recently who speak of the occasions when he came to preach in the chapels there as

**Isaac in Nigeria with Mac and Sylvia and their children Paul, Oliver and the Author, Sarah.**

**A Whit Monday service at Gwennap Pit.**

unforgettable days. For my part I can remember wanting to rise and applaud and cheer when he had finished.

He loved to go to the more remote chapels of Devon and Cornwall to preach and was still attending and participating in such services during the last ten years of his life. A couple who live on the edge of Bodmin Moor say they can remember him in his younger days arriving bare-back on a horse to preach nearby. I could not help wondering whether he came without a saddle because he was so absent minded that he had forgotten to harness the horse or whether he just found it more comfortable.

Two months before I was born in June 1939 my grandfather preached at the famous annual Whit Monday Service at Gwennap Pit — the Cornish amphitheatre cut into the side of Carn Marth near Redruth — which has perfect acoustics and it was here that Wesley preached to twenty thousand people. I would have loved to hear my grandfather's sermon on that day to the huge open-air congregation.

He was also to conduct a service in 1957 at the Cornish Methodist shrine, Trewint. This is the cottage, near Altarnun on the edge of

Bodmin Moor, which was visited by John Wesley and his fellow preachers during the eighteenth century and in which they were welcomed and returned to preach from on many of their Westcountry travels. In 1950 the cottage was re-opened having been carefully restored by the Trewint Trust which was formed by Stanley Sowton who had retired to Rilla Mill after a life-time of energetic service at the headquarters of the Methodist Missionary Society.

My grandfather, speaking at Trewint said, 'These rooms now restored will stand for 500 years as a memorial to John Wesley — and Stanley Sowton.' On Wesley Day every year a crowd gathers at the cottage for an open air service and about 3,000 people visit the rooms every year.

Olive Venning, that trusted family friend, used to drive him to his speaking engagements during his last years when he could not drive himself. She remembers a particular occasion at Temple in the heart of Bodmin Moor. The chapel had been closed and it was decided it should be re-opened and to have a Harvest Festival. They arrived late having lost the way and Olive remembers, 'We drove up a very narrow lane to find half a dozen people waiting for us with candles. They were there for the ceremony of unlocking the doors and we went in to the dark chapel. Gradually more folk came bringing paraffin lamps. Inside was a copper for heating water and tables laid with china. As folks came they brought pasties, sandwiches, cakes, etc. for a feast after the service.

'We gradually saw the harvest decorations — a string of onions hung behind Mr Foot. A couple of old farmers sat each side of him and they lost no time in counting the collection when he had finished conducting the service. It was an occasion Mrs Foot and I always remembered and made us laugh whenever we thought of it.'

And on another occasion Mrs Venning remembers driving him to Blisland also in the heart of the Moor. 'There is a village green with houses all around and it was a glorious summer's day. The folk had brought out all their easy chairs to sit around the green and listen to the speech Mr Foot was to deliver. It was really a very quaint sight, but very enjoyable in the brilliant sunshine.'

His way of imparting his religious feelings to us was not in dreary silent Bible readings on serious meditating Sundays, but he would recite great chunks of the Bible in his rich and energetic voice. On Sundays he would sit at his beloved piano and strum out the tunes of the hymns half shouting and half singing the words, getting us children to join in and it was impossible not to be infected by his enthusiasm. His beloved dog, the Irish Setter Roddy joined in too — howling in a most terrifying way but it always gave my grandfather great pleasure.

His father, Isaac the elder, had also been a local Methodist preacher who travelled all over Devon speaking in the chapels. So from an early age he was used to and familiar with visiting many of the less known Westcountry chapels.

He would take terrific pains with his sermons writing out his notes and building slowly on his text until he was satisfied and just as he loved to preach himself so he enjoyed going to hear a good preacher and would rejoice for the rest of the day when he had heard a fine sermon.

I was always aware of the division between Chapel people and Church people and most of the Liberal people we knew in Cornwall were Methodists too. When I was a teenager I went to Italy and found myself worshipping in the Roman Catholic cathedrals and churches and loving the pomp and ritual, but I felt a vague feeling of guilt. Grandpa would not have approved. Those stark and not very beautiful chapels of the Westcountry, which my grandfather believed were the real backbone of Christianity and where I had first been taken to worship, a close, more earthly God, seemed far away. I felt he would scoff at my new reverence for incense and High Mass.

But when I later told him that I found it quite easy to enjoy services in Church of England churches, Italian Roman Catholic cathedrals or Methodist chapels, he merely pointed out that the closest relation between a congregation and God was offered in a Methodist context, what he called 'The freest and fullest access of the man to his maker', and I saw it to be true.

The chapels of the Westcountry made by working men, inspired by John Wesley, from their carefully saved hard earned income moved him as much as the cathedrals and the spires of the parish churches. But he was not immune to beauty and he too travelled on the continent admiring the fine architecture of the grand churches.

When his great friend, Lawrence Maker of Callington, wrote a book about the Methodist chapels of Cornwall called *Cob and Moorstone* he contributed the foreword. In it he wrote, 'These buildings, especially those erected in earlier years, have behind them a story of romance and sacrifice not less inspiring than that which tells of the cathedrals and the glorious parish churches. These places, often plain and severely simple were erected mainly by the sacrifice of the peasantry and labouring folk. In the earliest days, certainly, they were built by the pence of the poor. Simple they had to be. In a certain sense they were the effort of homeless folk who felt they had somehow to get a roof over their heads. Here, it may be, is no tower or gleaming spire, here the traveller will not find

*The high embowèd roof*
*With antique pillars massy proof*
*And storied windows richly dight*
*Casting a dim religious light.*

' . . . A hundred years ago Thomas Carlyle, it will be remembered, went with Emerson for a walk over the long hills near Craigenputtock. They sat down, and talked of the immortality of the soul. "Christ died upon a tree", said Carlyle, "and that built Dunscore Kirk yonder." Everyone of these Methodist churches has the same foundation whatever may be the date carved upon its stones.'

In the beginning was the Word and as far as my grandfather was concerned in the beginning the Word came alive through the Bible. He was following in a true Methodist tradition — learn and read your Bible.

I have often been amazed at the power of expression amongst Westcountry Methodists, especially amongst some of the older ones who have had little education. And then I realised that their varied vocabulary, their strong phrases, their captivating eloquence all come from knowing their Bible almost by heart and from listening to some really fine preaching over the years. It is a special kind of Bible-talk that is explicit but full of warmth and colour. Some may have lacked adequate classroom education but the Sunday school and Bible classes had filled a large gap.

As my grandfather said himself in a broadcast in 1938 on 'The Bible in Personal Life', 'The peasant or the artisan who read his Bible and studied the word from day to day, became inevitably, in some degree, a man of cultivated mind . . . Let us take one illustration — George Loveless — the leader of the Tolpuddle Martyrs. This man, a hundred years ago, was sentenced to years of transportation. He was a farm labourer, earning a few shillings a week. He is now being recognised as a great man, and the centenary of his martyrdom was recently celebrated with high public honours. When people now read his letters, or his defence spoken in the dock, they are astonished. Where did this disinherited village labourer get his style — the noble simplicity of his diction, and the majesty of his phrase? The answer is simple. This unschooled peasant was a devout student of the Bible. As with many another, in him was the mighty combination of the sincere mind, the open book, and the Grace of God.'

In the same broadcast he reckoned, 'The Englishman without his Bible is deprived of one half of his inheritance.'

But as well as being a basis for education he saw the Bible as a living message and often referred to it as the Book of Hope. He kept reading his Bible until he died and was astounded that 'often the page that is most familiar, and has been read a hundred times, is suddenly lit up with new meaning, and this new interpretation often springs from one's own experience'.

He would often quote something his friend Sir Arthur Quiller Couch had said about the Bible: 'It is in everything we see, hear, feel, because it is in our blood.'

On a lighter note when he was preparing a speech about the Bible one of my aunts offered to type out the proof for him. As he often did when the typed copy returned he read it out to the assembled family. 'How often', he read, 'do you see someone reading their Bible in a public convenience?' . . . Of course it had been wrongly typed; it was meant to read 'public conveyance'. The whole family collapsed in laughter and he could be heard for some days chuckling and muttering under his breath, 'How often do you see someone reading their Bible in a public convenience?' The joke like so many others remained a family favourite which he would often repeat. And once again one could see that those things that were dearest to his heart and which he took most seriously were still capable of making him laugh and being gently ridiculed.

Often when writing or telegramming his children on some particular occasion my grandfather would merely name a chapter and verse from the Bible. He always seemed to have the perfect quotation at his finger tips. Once when my father was Governor of Cyprus and the situation there was at its worst my grandfather telegrammed him, 'See Second Corinthians, Chapter four verses eight and nine.' When my father looked up the text it read, 'We are troubled on every side, yet not distressed; we are perplexed, but not in despair; persecuted but not forsaken; cast down but not destroyed.' What pleased and surprised my grandfather was that my father was able to cap his text and sent back a telegram, 'See Romans five, Chapter five, verses three and four.' It read, 'And not only so, but we glory in tribulations also; knowing that tribulation worketh patience; and patience, experience; and experience hope.'

My father was the only one of the seven children who remained faithful to the Methodist form of worship and still goes to chapel regularly. Early on in his career when he was promoted and sent as Colonial Secretary to Jamaica he telegrammed his father to tell him the good news and he recorded, 'I eagerly waited to receive his reply. I looked forward to his congratulations. I even hoped for a word of commendation. How well I remember opening his telegram which read, "Glad about your move to Jamaica. There is a strong Methodist community there".'

Although my grandfather's children were all successful in their own fields and all blessed with high intelligence and all inherited their father's love for literature, my grandmother was always saddened that none of them was good enough to be a Methodist Minister.

Of all the characters of the Bible who fired my grandfather's imagination the Apostle Paul and the translator Tyndale were his favourites. At the time of the celebrations of the four hundredth anniversary of the Reformation he wrote a pamphlet about William Tyndale whom he called 'An Apostle of England'.

He admired greatly the sacrifice Tyndale made in accomplishing his lifetime's ambition to translate the New Testament. He was forced into exile and then fled from one place to another until in Worms, the city made famous by Luther's historic challenge, the printing was finished in 1535 and the first printed English New Testament was produced. Tyndale had said to his clerical opponents, 'I defy the Pope and all his laws. If God spare my life, ere many years, I will cause a boy that driveth the plough shall know more of the Scriptures than thou doest.' These sentiments were enough to make my grandfather Tyndale's fervent admirer. He had studied everything about Tyndale's life and was forever impressed that a man should suffer so greatly for his ideals, never

**Lord Caradon as Sir Hugh Foot, Governor of Jamaica.** ▶

compromising but working towards the translation of both the Old and New Testaments and then finding a way of circulating the English translations in the land from which he had been exiled and was never allowed back. That Tyndale spent his last years in a prison outside Brussels begging for a candle and his Bible and his Hebrew Grammar and was eventually strangled and burned at the stake in a public execution increased my grandfather's admiration for his hero. And that, not long after Tyndale's death, the translation of the Bible was accepted officially into Britain made his hero's suffering seem all the more significant. He knew where to visit the Tyndale statue on the Embankment by the Thames and found the inscription beneath most fitting: 'And this is the record, that God hath given unto us eternal life, and this life is in his Son.'

In 1937 Isaac Foot was made Vice President of the Methodist Conference, an honour he held more proudly than almost any other

**Left: Sir Dingle Foot Q.C.**
**Below: Isaac Foot at the 1958 Methodist Conference.**

he was to receive. In his address to the Conference he opened by saying, 'If I were in control of the arrangements I would have the session confined to the President's message and the "Hallelujah" chorus.' And then went on to make a lengthy but moving address full as always of quotations from his favourite literary and Biblical figures. In this speech he also paid tribute to his parents, his father who had been a Methodist preacher for sixty years and his mother of whom he said, 'She had a beautiful voice and it was her singing in the choir of the Methodist Chapel in Plymouth that first attracted my father's attention.

'. . . To the last my mother led the singing in Chapel because, becoming rather deaf in her older years, she generally led off the first note before the choir. She had in earlier years a hard time trying to train her five sons and two daughters, and her discipline was severe, but in her later days she became all gentleness, all fragrance, and all grace. Barrie said, "The God to whom little boys say their prayers has a face very like their mother's." I expect most of us here have found that to be true.'

He ended the address with a challenge. 'With the recovery of that confidence Methodism can conquer this generation for Jesus Christ, and can express itself as did Foch to Joffre in August 1914: "My right has been rolled up: my left has been driven back: my centre has been smashed. I have ordered an advance in all directions." It was that confident challenge that recalls the fearless words of the man whom I have frequently quoted today (St Paul) three cubits in stature he touched the sky. "For the weapons of our warfare are not carnal, but mighty through God to the pulling down of strongholds. Casting down imaginations and every high thing that exalteth itself against the knowledge of God and bringing into captivity every thought to the obedience of Christ." '

He seemed to know by heart every word the Apostle Paul wrote. Mr David Hawken told me that when he was a boy preacher he went to make one of his first sermons in the West End Chapel in Callington. 'When I got into the pulpit I looked across at the congregation and saw Isaac Foot sitting there. My heart sank, but I have studied well my text and it was about St Paul. I will tell them all I know about the Apostle, I thought. When the service was over Mr Foot came to the vestry to congratulate me and ask me if I would like a lift home. I said I had my bicycle but thanked him kindly. It was only a few days later that I read that Mr Foot was

70

probably the greatest living authority on St Paul. I was quite overcome.'

As always my grandfather had a joke to tell about Callington Chapel. Apparently a member of the congregation had been so shocked when a harmonium had been introduced to the chapel that he had left and gone to the church. When it was discovered the seniors of the chapel had asked him to come and explain his actions. The gentleman had arrived to meet the gathering and they asked him, 'Why is it any different to attend a church which has an organ than to come to the chapel with a harmonium?' Without a second thought the man replied, 'There is a great deal of difference between an organ in a church and an harmonium in the House of God.'

When Isaac died the then President of the Methodist Conference, the Reverend Edward Rogers, paid tribute to him at his Memorial Service at the Methodist Central Hall in Plymouth. After speaking about the 'Wide disparity of his interests, the enormous range of his concerns and his curiosity about life' he said, 'he treated me for my own good as a promising but rather headstrong young son. As he told me more than once he had plenty of practice in that direction.'

But what touched me most in that service was the lesson read by his nephew, David Foot Nash. Taken from 1 Corinthians XIII the words seemed the most fitting that anyone could have chosen for that occasion. And it was taken from Tyndale's 1534 revision for which he had such reverence.

'Though I speak with the tongues of men and angels, and yet had no love, I were even as a sounding brass, or as a tinkling cymbal. And though I could prophesy, and understood all secrets, and all knowledge; yea, if I had all faith so that I could move mountains out of their places, and yet had no love, I were nothing. And though I bestowed all my goods to feed the poor, and though I gave my body, even that I burned, and yet had no love, it profiteth me nothing.'

It reminded me and made me realise, not for the first time, that it was not his knowledge, or his gift of speaking with 'the tongues of men and angels' or his understanding, or even his faith which had so endeared him to us all. It was, without a doubt, his great love for people and for life itself that had been easily his most outstanding quality.

# V

# His Books

*For Books are not absolutely dead things but doe*
*contain a potencie of life in them to be as active as*
*that soule was whose progeny they are.*

*MILTON*

My grandfather's great weakness was for books.

He would buy a whole library of books, if it was necessary to do so, to obtain just one book he had been looking for. I know my grandmother often despaired when he went up to London to attend a Liberal meeting. She knew that the likelihood was that he would also attend a book auction or spend sometime browsing through second-hand book shops, never returning without some acquisition.

He once said, 'A library book has never meant much to me. If a book is of interest I want it for my very own. I want it for the second reading, perhaps the third, or the fourth. I want it with my name in it, with my own mark and symbols and underlinings and references.'

Pencrebar bulged with books. The library, the most popular room in the house where a fire was always lit from morning to night, was lined with books from ceiling to floor. But he knew where each book was and would often break off in the middle of a conversation to reach for one, or climb his little ladder to find the volume he needed, never for a moment hesitating in finding the exact one he wanted.

In this room he did all his reading never minding what confusion went on around him. We could be having heated discussions, be listening to the wireless, or playing games on the floor, he never seemed to find it distracting. Under his anglepoise lamp he sat, puffing at his pipe, rising every now and then with a grunt to knock it out on the granite fireplace, returning unabashed to his reading throwing only a glance or some quip in our direction. I think he actually enjoyed being surrounded by the young and we were never told to leave him in peace or 'run along and play'.

To get to the lavatory you had to climb over stacks of books; up the back stairs to the attic they were piled; in the laundry room where the old fashioned boiler was fixed to the middle of the floor books were stacked everywhere and for as long as I can remember, that room was no longer used for its original purpose but was yet another place to store the books. One of the front facing bedrooms was called the Greek Testament room after the 450 volumes it housed and each part of the house meant something special to my grandfather because of the author's works which were kept in them. Often you would find people sitting down in the passage or on the stairs having found a book they had always wanted to read, starting to browse through it and soon forgetting where they were.

My grandfather was educated in Plymouth at Plymouth Public School, where he recorded he paid twopence a week for the privilege, and then later at the Hoe Grammar School. About his school days,

**The library at Pencrebar: 'My grandfather's great weakness was for books . . .'**

he recorded, 'The classes were very large and sometimes 80 or 100 of us would be committed to the charge of some unfortunate single teacher. I remember very little of what I was taught but I suppose I learned something. Emerson says somewhere that "we send boys to the schoolmaster but it is their schoolfellows who teach them". Certainly I learned a great deal from my schoolmates.'

It was in his Sunday school room at Wesley in Plymouth that his love for poetry was born when he heard Macaulay's *Horatius* being recited. But most of his knowledge and education was self-taught and went on until the day he died.

His thirst and capacity for knowledge was something that continued to amaze all those who knew him. In a moving broadcast he once gave on collecting books he told of his father giving him a gift of five sovereigns when he was a lad which was placed in a savings account in the bank. He told how he went and took the money from the bank to buy some books he had seen in a second-hand book shop, and how frightened he was to declare his action to his family. This was only the first of many such occasions. As long as he lived he went on buying books, often which he could not afford, later which he could not house. The surveyor looking over Pencrebar when I was still a child told him severely, 'Place one more book in this house Mr Foot and I cannot be responsible for the outcome.'

In the attic of the house there were five rooms once used as studies for the five sons. They were wonderful places to go and often as a child I would climb the back stairs and sit in the little room that had been my father's bedroom and study and look out over the steeply sloping field and the woods beyond and across the valley to the farm on the opposite bank.

There was a special sort of atmosphere of mustiness from old books and worn carpets and spiders' webs and it was the room where the treasures I could not cart around the world were kept. So I would go and unwrap my little parcels of half forgotten china ornaments and well thumbed copies of much loved Beatrix Potter books and outgrown toys so full of nostalgia. It was a place where you could get away from everyone if you felt like being alone and you could sit and think without interruption. It was never a frightening place. In fact I never felt threatened at all anywhere in that big old friendly house.

I could imagine what a good place those little studies had been to sit and learn when my father and his brothers had all been at Oxford or Cambridge. Here they had been able to keep their treasures and their books. Here in the special hush of the attic they could sit at their work and give themselves over to the love of learning their father had so inspired in them. My grandfather had never had such perfect studying places. A lot of his learning had taken place as he walked to work from the time when he was a young man working as a clerk in London to when he lived at St Cleer and walked to Liskeard station in the morning to catch his train to Plymouth where he had set up his solicitor's practice.

He had not had the privilege of a university education and yet I don't imagine there was ever a time when his sons, who all went to Oxford or Cambridge, could outwit him. But they did bring their knowledge from their public schools and their universities back to him. He had given my father extra pocket money to teach him his school boy Greek so that he could read the *New Testament* in the original, and not long after he died I found, when sorting out some of his papers, a book of Wordsworth's Poetical Works that his youngest son Christopher had given him having won it as a school prize in 1931. Written in his own handwriting it says, 'This book Christopher gave me, October 1949'.

Books were to him the loveliest things in the world, but he was very generous with them giving them as presents on special occasions to mark the importance of the event, although he often wrote in the inscription that he gave the book with regret.

From early on he was aware that I would never be the brightest grandchild. But not deterred he watched to see which way my interests lay. The first book he ever gave me, when I was five years old, was a beautifully illustrated, handsomely bound volume of stories about cats, after I had confessed to him that they were my favourite animals. He knew that this way he would encourage my slow reading and would thus stimulate my love for books. And he was right for I still have the book and still read it with pleasure.

Years later when I was about thirteen I was staying with him and he was horrified to find that I was not avidly reading anything. He gave me a beautiful early copy of the *Prisoner of Zenda*. For the next two days I never put the book down, complaining when I was called for meals or asked to perform some helpful task. Curled up on the large brown sofa in front of the fire in the library I would occasionally lift my eyes to watch him where he sat in his familiar chair deep in reading. And once I caught his eye and heard him chuckle as I complained about being called to lunch — he knew he had won the battle against the illiteracy of his granddaughter. As soon as I had finished the *Prisoner of Zenda* he handed me *Rupert of Hentzau* and I read on.

He never stopped encouraging me although some of his other grandchildren were far more worth his trouble. When I was sixteen and went to Italy and fell in love with Florence he was delighted and once more showered me with books about the city and the artists who had painted and sculpted there and about whom I showed such an interest. When I told him about my travels around Tuscany and later to Milan and Venice he went in search of more books, looking to the bottom of the piles in the laundry room and on the stairs and in the cloakroom and came back with more and more wonderful volumes.

It was remarkable that he showed this interest in all his grandchildren. Giving them and lending them books he knew would be of particular interest to them. But his favourite grandchild was his daughter Jennifer's eldest child Alison. It was she he would draw on to his knee when she was very small and stroking her silky hair murmur, 'Dear maid, dear maid'. Their devotion for each other lasted until he died and she would often go to visit him in the holidays and wrote to him regularly telling him what she was reading, which of her studies were interesting her and always ending by saying how much she longed to be at Pencrebar.

After my grandfather's eightieth birthday in 1960 she wrote him and Kitty from her school in Bristol and here is an extract:

*I hope I will be able to come to the Cromwell dinner. In my Bible readings the other day they had a saying by Cromwell to the Scottish Presbyterians: 'I beseech you by the mercy of Jesus Christ to conceive it possible that ye may be mistaken'.*

*Miss Mackenzie, our English Mistress, said I did an excellent English exam question on Thomas Hardy, which I am very pleased about, as I like him very much. However, I have read most of his good books. I think 'The Return of the Native' is almost the best and then maybe 'Jude the Obscure'...*

*The other day two of our mistresses did a debate on the African Boycott. Then we voted on it, but most of the school were against it. I think it is quite a good thing, as it shows we sympathise with*

Isaac Foot with his second wife, Kitty, and his granddaughter,
Alison, Jennifer's eldest child.

*the Africans. I enjoyed Doctor Zhivago very much. I think I told
you I was reading it in my last letter. I hope you are both keeping
very well and having a nice time at Pencrebar. Please also give my
love to Uncle Chris when you see him next.*
*With lots of love and kisses*
*thinking of you always*
*Ally.*

Ten years before Isaac had used the same quote of Cromwell's
that his granddaughter now was learning. He was incensed by an
attack the Lord Bishop of London had made on Cromwell and had
written an open letter to the Bishop which was published in *The
Observer* on Sunday 20 February 1949 and ended with those lines of
Cromwell's.

Alison needed little encouragement in her reading and was always
bright beyond her years and in tune not only with his literary
thoughts but with his idealistic beliefs. Although she was a lot
younger than I was I always treated her with respect for the
happiness she brought him, and for her astute mind which was able
to contend with his.

In September 1960, three months before he died, I became
engaged and my fiancé and I went to stay with him. He passed his
beautiful, long, slim hands along the serried ranks of books in the
library, looking for something appropriate to mark the occasion. To
my husband he gave Joseph Conrad's *Almayer's Folly* and to me
*Alps and Sanctuaries* by Samuel Butler. Both were first editions,
and both were perfectly suited to the recipients.

The last time I saw him, a few weeks before he died, he was in bed
and already weak but as cheerful and gay and full of jokes as ever. I
climbed on to the eiderdown beside him and he patted my hand with
his and drew me near. 'Now what are you reading my dear,' he said,
always one of the first questions he asked us. I hesitated a moment
having had a busy few weeks working in London — the truth was I
was not reading anything. He laughed realising my predicament
and tapped me playfully on the back of the head and said with
resigned amusement, 'I suppose it takes all kinds to make a world.'
But it dumbfounded him that anyone, least of all a grandchild of his,
could at any time, no matter what the circumstances, not be deeply
involved in reading something or other. There had never been, I felt
sure, a day in his life when he had not read something of value.

His library was said to be the largest in Britain collected by one man in his lifetime. There were some 70,000 books. When he died the library was sold as a whole to the University of California, and though it was spread through several campuses it was to remain known as the Isaac Foot Library.

But it was not the size so much that impressed people, it was the remarkable breadth of interests shown. There were works on Cromwell and Milton, a fantastic collection of Bibles, 450 Greek Testaments alone, books on the Apostles especially Paul, and a group of religious books concerned with the Wesleyans, showing the strong influence Methodism played in his life. There were 2,000 books on the French revolution and Napoleon Bonaparte, and several volumes covering the American Civil War, military campaigns and Abraham Lincoln, another hero of his. There were books covering the Italian Renaissance and the works of Robert Louis Stevenson, Thomas Carlyle and William Wordsworth.

Writing about his library after it was sold Aubrey Pryor in the *Western Morning News* of 20 August 1965 said: 'Quite simply, this magnificent library corroborates the opinion formed of Isaac Foot in his native Westcountry, where he was known to be an expert collector, a man of aesthetic sensibilities and a scholar.

'Although it would be difficult to say which of these characteristics is predominant, it is doubtless his scholarship which is most easily discernible.'

To me the amazing thing remained that he had known and loved each one so well. Every book bore his own Ex Libris plate and was heavily marked in pencil in his most distinctive handwriting.

Mr David Hawken remembers that when the Liberal Rallies were held at Pencrebar and thousands of people came from all over Cornwall the house was always left open and people were allowed to wander where they would. He never lost a single book and was delighted if anyone showed any interest in the library offering to lend books to whoever asked. These volumes were there to be read and marvelled at, their monetary value was of little interest to him except when he needed or wanted to buy more.

Mr Robert Kitson of Morval wrote in a special edition of *Spotlight on Cornwall* after my grandfather's death the following letter:

*It was only in his latter years that I came to know Isaac Foot personally. In so many matters we were poles apart. He was*

**Left: Michael Foot who wrote *The Pen and the Sword*. Below: Isaac Foot's inscription in the book he gave to the Author on her engagement.**

To my
granddaughter
Sarah Dingle Foot
from Isaac Foot.

ALPS AND SANCTUARIES.

19 September, 1960.

*chapel, teetotal and a model of self-discipline. My background was so entirely different. Yet he had the humanity and real wisdom never to criticise, always to tolerate. I first met him at my Grandmother's funeral in 1942; he came to Morval Church unannounced and alone, to pay tribute to one with whom in Plymouth affairs he had been generally opposed, but for whom he had the highest respect — which was wholeheartedly reciprocated. They were antagonists but in the old way, in which honour and admiration was freely conceded.*

*When I ceased my flirtation with the Conservative Party, left the National Liberals and openly re-associated myself with the Bodmin Liberal Party, he never gave me any strictures. On the contrary, he offered me hospitality, help and that gentle kind of encouragement which only the old who are really wise can proffer to the impetuous.*

*I have had Liberal Fetes at Morval and the house has been opened to guided and organised parties. However Isaac Foot when he held similar functions at his home threw it completely open and trusted that none of his priceless books would be taken. As far as I am aware his faith in people was never broken.*

*Faith was the foundation of his life. Even if his attitude often seemed by present day standards narrow and confined; even if sometimes his actions were as if the Civil War of 300 years ago was still being fought, he was essentially a large man, a man of faith, with a wide grasp of human problems. We in South East Cornwall have lost a father figure, but Britain as a whole has lost a symbol of the days of unselfish service, and the principle of 'love thy neighbour' which he personified.*

*I took my eight year old son to Isaac Foot's Memorial Service in Plymouth. The name meant little to him, but one day he will say with pride: 'my father took me to Isaac Foot's Memorial Service'.*

*I have the honour to be, Sir,*
       *Your obedient Servant,*
       *R.R.B. Kitson.*

But characteristically my grandfather had a story to tell about his library that made all who heard it laugh.

One day when walking in Callington he met a gentleman who had just taken a book from the town library. 'What are you reading?' asked Isaac. The gentleman showed him his book and told my grandfather how much he enjoyed reading. 'You must come and see my library at Pencrebar one day soon,' he said.

Accordingly a date was set and the gentleman arrived at Pencrebar. As my grandfather led him, from room to room his visitor was speechless marvelling at the shelves upon shelves of priceless volumes. Eventually he got his voice back and remarked, 'I don't expect there is a finer library in all Callington.'

He himself only wrote one book though he had several pamphlets published, notably a major work comparing the ideals and sayings of his two great idols Cromwell and Lincoln.

He was inordinately proud when in 1957 his son Michael wrote *The Pen and the Sword* about Jonathan Swift and the Duke of Marlborough. In his acknowledgements in the book Uncle Michael wrote: 'My father encouraged me to write this book and he has supplied me with much information, his own notes on the subject and many volumes from his library.'

But my grandfather's own little book was inspired by the story of an ardent Methodist, Michael Verran of Callington — a miner of the nineteenth century who performed a self sacrificing feat in saving his fellow miner during an accident in the mine and whose own life was saved by a seeming miracle. By some chance Thomas Carlyle read in the newspaper of the event and with the help of Caroline Fox managed to raise money so that Verran could become a farmer and no longer return to the arduous mining life.

The story held for him many pleasures — it brought together the life of a working Methodist and a learned man of letters and a selfless deed done in the name of God, and it took place in and around his home town of Callington.

My uncles say that his interests were changing too quickly for him to sit down and write a book of any length himself. He was far too busy reading, even in his last years.

My Uncle Michael once said that he thought his father would have been happy to spend the whole of his life reading. It was my grandmother who would say to him, 'Come along now, the world is waiting to be saved.'

# VI

# Plymouth

*Turris fortissima est nomen Jehova.*
*Plymouth's Motto*

My grandfather was a true and proud son of Plymouth. His roots were founded there at his birth 100 years ago in 1880 and he was brought up, educated and lived there for the first twenty years of his married life.

In 1909 my grandfather opened his solicitor's practice in Plymouth in partnership with Edgar Bowden and worked there throughout the First War having been turned down on medical grounds for military service. He was left to hold the fort at his office spending quite a time defending conscientious objectors, not always a popular task.

He loved and knew Plymouth as well as anyone else and once broadcast his early reminiscences of the City.

'I was born in Plymouth at No 10 Notte Street, in a house my father had built two years before. Behind it was the workshop he had also built and with its three storeys with timbers and materials of all kinds.'

It was not until 1927 when my grandfather was 47 and all his seven children had been born that he moved to his eventual home in Cornwall, Pencrebar near Callington. For a time during the First War the family moved to Ramsland a pretty house on the edge of Bodmin Moor at St Cleer. It was then that he lost his heart to Cornwall and so to us grandchildren Plymouth and Cornwall were always inextricably mixed in our affections through his great love for both.

But he was always ready to joke about the age old differences between Cornwall and Devon. His old friend Mr Arthur Blight of Callington told me recently that my grandfather had once asked him, 'Do you know the difference between a man from Devon and one from Cornwall?' 'I had no time to reply', Mr Blight told me, 'before he said, "A man from Devon when he leaves your home looks around to see if there is anything he has left behind, whereas a Cornishman when he leaves your home looks around to see if there is anything worth taking".' Mr Blight said, 'He was making a dig at me since I was born in Callington and he was born in Plymouth.'

In November 1945 he was made Lord Mayor of Plymouth and it was during this year of office that my grandmother died. My grandmother had been taken to hospital in East Grinstead for an operation and my grandfather went with her. After the operation, on being told that all was well, he caught a train back to Plymouth where he was to attend an official function — but a message was delivered to him when the train stopped at Reading. My grandmother was failing. By the time he got back to the hospital she was gone. Somehow his duties as Lord Mayor seemed to help him through this terrible time of grief. His old friend Lawrence Spear's wife became his Lady Mayoress and the friendship of this couple was obviously a great help to him at this time.

His lifelong love affair with Plymouth came to its fruition when he became Lord Mayor and he impressed upon us children then and for years later the romance of his home town. Even in childhood it was the historical connotations of the town which so appealed to him. He said of Notte Street, 'As a birthplace it was the one I should have chosen before all other . . . it was the one street along which must have walked all the men whose names were most closely identified with the fame of Plymouth in past years. Along that street must have walked Humphrey Gilbert, Sir John Hawkins, Sir Francis Drake, Martin Frobisher, Sir Walter Raleigh, Admiral Robert Blake and in later years Captain Cooke and Admiral Nelson.'

Just the thought of such men passing along the street where he lived fired his imagination. But of course by the time he was born and living in Notte Street things had changed. 'The main impression', he recorded in 1951 'left upon my mind as I look back upon the Notte Street of nearly 70 years ago is that I lived in the midst of a multitude of people. Every house and indeed almost

**Isaac Foot's parents, Isaac the elder and Eliza.▶**

every room seemed full of people.'

And apparently gang warfare was rife in those days. 'High Street', he said, 'which ran uphill at right angles at the bottom (of Notte Street) was not so important as Notte Street but when hostilities commenced these courtyards of theirs provided powerful auxiliaries. During one of these battles I have seen the High Street army sweep Notte Street clear from the bottom to the top. The victors would then encamp in triumph, sometimes around an impoverished fire fed with the weapons taken from the enemy. Meanwhile the defeated Notte Streeters took refuge in their homes, nursing their wounds. That was literally true, for sometimes there was actual bloodshed.

'On these bigger occasions no policeman ever came in sight, nothing but a body of police could have coped with that formidable situation.'

Notte Street had another special interest for my grandfather. His father also built the Mission Hall there on the opposite side of the road from their home which was completed in 1883. His father bought the house and garden which had been occupied by William Cookworthy, the great chemist of Plymouth of porcelain fame, and there out of his own resources built the Hall. He was careful to preserve the pediment of Cookworthy which had been above the front door.

My grandfather's very earliest memory was of visiting the Mission Hall when it was being built and he described it thus:

'I couldn't have been more than three years of age at the time and I recall my father taking me in his arms and stepping from joist to joist on the first floor of that building and everyone worrying. He held me very close, I was frightened and I remember when he finished this, what I thought was a perilous journey, all the workmen who were there in the crowd joined in the cheer.'

Later the Hall was destroyed in the blitz of 1941 during the Second World War, as was most of Notte Street.

As a boy my grandfather walked to and from Plymouth Public School twice a day. Six days a week he did the walk, up St Andrew's

◄ **Looking down Hoegate Street to Notte Street where Isaac the Elder's workshop still stands on the left hand corner.**

Street, past St Andrew's Church, into the Old Town Street, along Saltash Street. The excitement in Saltash Street was that it led to the sugar refinery and sometimes when the wagons passed laden with sacks of raw sugar one of the more daring of the school boys would cut a hole in the bottom corner of a sack. As my grandfather pointed out, 'It was petty larceny, of course, but the driver in front had his horses to look after and each one of us filled his pockets with rough brown sugar as his rightful share of the spoils.'

So Isaac Foot, always known as a Puritan in later years, was as much up to childish pranks as any of his other school mates. One of his great friends at school was a boy called Lovell Redmore Dunstan who became Lord Mayor of Plymouth in 1920. As children they often joined together in their boyhood adventures which were not always of a guiltless nature.

My grandfather remembered extremely clearly escaping a close brush with the law at the very early age of six years old. It was in the Autumn of 1886 and he and his friends had been preparing their Guy Fawkes in his father's workshop. It was the custom that the Notte Street boys burned their Guy Fawkes on Plymouth Hoe. But the news came that a new order of the Police forbade the use of the Hoe for any burning of any Guy Fawkes and as he recorded, 'We held a council of war and it was decided that police or no police Guy Fawkes was to be burned and burned on Plymouth Hoe. We made one concession to law and order. We decided to burn it, not on the brow of the Hoe by Drake's statue but on the edge of the quarries on the west end of the Hoe.

' . . . I, at the age of six, was the youngest of the party. My advice was not sought but although frightened I fully approved. Two or three of our members carried the Guy and then we all assembled in the darkness at the edge of the quarries at about ten o'clock on the fateful night. Because of my age I was deputed to keep watch and to give the alarm at once on seeing any policeman. The Guy lighted gloriously and the blaze was in full vigour and it was at that point that I saw something approaching me. It was the clasp of the policeman's belt. Fortunately I gave the alarm in time. The older malefactors, and amongst them three of my brothers, determined that whatever happened Guy Fawkes was not to be captured. He was flung high in the air and by sheer good fortune came down dead straight on his sharp spike in a position almost inaccessible amongst the quarry rocks.

88

'The Police were busy trying to make captures so Guy Fawkes burned down to the stump and with the squibs he spat defiance to the last. The rockets roared rebellion against our local tyrants. Two of our number were caught. They spent the night in the police station. I eluded capture and ran home like a hare. I went to bed very quietly to avoid parental enquiry. The merest chance saved me from being held up before the town next morning as a dreadful example of juvenile delinquency.'

This story gave us children the greatest pleasure. It was marvellous to think of our law abiding grandfather caught in such treacherous activities.

Notte Street lies between the Barbican and the Hoe. From here he could walk down to the Quays and watch the boats coming and going, a favourite pastime of his and his school mates. As he said, 'It meant long hours sitting on the sun-warmed slabs of the Sutton Wharf with our legs dangling over the side fishing for crabs with a long piece of string and bait carefully selected from the great bins which the fishermen left.'

On other days he and his friends were up on the Hoe, walking around the Citadel, standing beneath the statue of Sir Francis Drake, playing football, flying kites. This was on the days before there was a restaurant or promenades or asphalt roads. He carefully instilled in us the magic and glory of that beautiful part of Plymouth so that when I stand there now looking out to the wide expanse of the wonderful harbour it is not Drake's drum I hear beating but the echo of the sound of his rich enthusiastic voice extolling us to appreciate the wonders of that grand place which had once been his childhood playground.

When he moved to a richer surburban area at the age of ten he missed the intimacy of Notte Street. As he said, 'In Notte Street I seemed to know everybody and everybody knew me. Now each residence was self-contained and next door neighbours seemed utter strangers. I felt sometimes almost an alien, an intruder, and every now and again I would slip back to old haunts.'

Recently I went to look at the small remaining part of my great grandfather's workshop — all that is left of the buildings he erected in Notte Street. Though things have changed so much I could imagine what a wonderful place it must have been to spend an early childhood. So close to the sea on one hand, and the great outlook of the Hoe above. It was easy to see how the romance of Plymouth gripped my grandfather's heart at an early age from this vantage point.

By the time he was twenty-one his family lived in another house built by his father called Ladywell. Up a quiet lane, not far from Greenbank Hospital, it must have been a most romantic house though it now has become somewhat neglected and converted into several flats. With its high ceilings, all beautifully plastered, with the coloured Victorian glass and the wrought iron balcony, the house and adjoining cottage were built round a courtyard with a long and beautiful conservatory leading from the street door to the front door of the house.

It was here in the 1920s that the huge Foot Christmas parties were always held. Sometimes there were sixty members of the family gathered there for their Christmas dinner. Stanley Goodman, a nephew of Isaac, remembers the occasions clearly. My grandfather was always the one to dress up as Father Christmas

**Ladywell House in Plymouth built by Isaac the Elder as the family home.**

with a huge white beard and wig.

Presents were piled at one end of the room and Isaac in his disguise would call out the names and each child would go and collect his present. Stanley told me that sometimes the procedure was a little daunting, especially when they were very young, as there was the danger of being landed with the forfeit present. This had been wrapped in hundreds of bits of paper and sealed with sealing wax and if you were landed with one it meant you had to open it in the middle of the room in sight of everyone with much clapping and cheering.

After the ritual of present opening the family would take it in turn to sing around the piano. My grandfather always sang his favourite song, *To Be a Farmers Boy,* and each member of the family would be encouraged to sing something of their choice.

It was also here that my grandfather's twenty-first birthday party was given and the following is a copy of the invitations sent out for the occasion:

**In** Ye Olden Times it was ye custome when the Youthe attayned ye age of Twentie-One Yeares, for his manic Friendes to gather togethere to make merrie, and wyshe him happynesse and muche joye. ✳ ✳ ✳ ✳

**Wherefore** in pursuance of ye said antient custome ISAAC FOOT, to wit, the Younger, who doth on Friday ye twentie-second of February, in the Yeare of our Lord, One Thousand Nine Hundred and One, legally pass from ye state of Infancie into that of Manhood doth invite

*Mr Robert Pile*

to a ryghte jovial gathering at "Ladie Welle" in ye Paryshe of Charles, in ye antient Townshype of Plymouth, at ye houre of thyrtie mynutes past six o'clock. ✳ ✳ ✳

Standing in that long conservatory the other day I could imagine the occasion and the family and friends arriving and walking along this glass covered way to be warmly greeted in the square and solid house built by Isaac, the elder. My admiration for my great grandfather's gift as a builder seemed to outweigh any pride I felt for the later accomplishments of the family in politics, diplomacy or the law. I remembered my grandfather telling us that although his father had workmen to help him there was not a single technique of building that he could not execute himself. From the sawing of wood to the making of bricks, he knew it all. The story goes that my great grandfather, Isaac the elder, as the family always referred to him, came from the little Devon village of Horrabridge, on the edge of Dartmoor, to Plymouth with £5 in his pocket; and there proceeded to set up his building, carpentering and undertaking business. He was a remarkable character in his own right, from all accounts, and a man of vision who believed implicitly in the power of prayer.

He not only built the Mission Hall in Notte Street but later a Hall for the Salvation Army in Plymouth with no visible means of financial help. When asked where he would obtain the money he said, 'I will pray for help.' And the help always came.

But it was his wife Eliza who managed to keep his practical affairs in some sort of order. Strange that a generation later my practical grandmother, Eva, was to keep her visionary Isaac under some sort of control.

In the *Western Morning News* of January 1969 the following story of Isaac the elder appeared:

'In the Devon village of Horrabridge one evening in the last quarter of the 19th century a group of 'tinners' from the then still functioning mines, somewhat mellow after slaking the silica with the local cider, saw the slim, slightly hunched figure of a Methodist teetotal carpenter walking by.

'One of them shouted, "Hey there Ikey, where's your monkey?" (the Italian organ grinder, crouched over his instrument, monkey on shoulder, was a familiar Victorian scene). The carpenter walked towards the merry miner and turned his back on him. "Jump up!" he said.' This is the earliest example I have heard of the verbal agility and the moral courage for which a most remarkable family is justly famed.

Only three years after his twenty-first birthday party in 1904, my grandfather was married and first set up house in Freedom Park

**Isaac and his family entertain the singer, Harry Lauder, at their Lipson Terrace home.**

Villas across the road from Ladywell House. A few years later they moved to Lipson Terrace where they were to live and bring up their first five children, Dingle, my father, John, Sally and Michael. Later Jennifer and Christopher were born at their house on Bodmin Moor.

He entered local politics as a Liberal Councillor for Greenbank Ward in 1907 and remained on the City Council for twenty years. He was appointed Deputy Mayor in 1920 and during this year of office he spent some time in the United States as Plymouth's representative at the Mayflower tercentenary, where his, by then fully developed gift for oratory was put to good use and he left an indelible impression behind him.

He was living at Pencrebar in Cornwall in 1945 when he was made Lord Mayor of Plymouth. He remembered vividly when he was a child the then Mayor of Plymouth visiting his school in full robes and because this had left such a lasting impression on him he vowed that he himself should so visit every school in Plymouth hoping to ignite civic pride and a love for local history in the minds of the children. Because of this practice of his he became known as 'the children's Lord Mayor'. At the Lord Mayor's reception of representative schoolchildren at Plymouth on 25 October 1946, Nancy Astor said to the children, 'Have a good, long look at your Lord Mayor, because you'll never see a Lord Mayor like him again.'

I remember him taking the grand robes from the cupboard where they hung in an upstairs passage at Pencrebar and showing them to us children with pride in his eyes.

I suppose his favourite Plymouthian character, or certainly the one he first brought alive in my mind's eye, was Sir Francis Drake who had also been Mayor of Plymouth in 1581. We all learned at a very early age the lines he so often recited to us and I can still hear my brother Paul at the age of five reciting in a clear high voice the words our grandfather made him learn by heart:

*Drake he was a Devon man, an' ruled the Devon seas*
*(Captain art thou sleepin' there below?)*
*Rovin' tho' his death fell, he went wi' heart at ease,*
*An' dreamin' arl the time of Plymouth Hoe*
*'Take my drum to England, hang it by the shore*
*Strike it when your powder's runnin' low*
*If the Dons sight Devon, I'll quit the port of Heaven*
*And drum them up the Channel as we drumm'd them long ago.*

He believed fervently in the legend that Drake's Drum could be heard beating at times of war and of victory. And he used this legend to colour a speech he broadcast to the Nation in the dark hours of 1940 when he had been asked to deliver a message of hope. The broadcast was entitled 'Drake's Drum Beats Again' and was a masterpiece of oratory, a rallying call to all those who might feel faint hearted. He quoted from Drake's letter to Walsingham at a time of national disaster:

'There must be a beginning of every matter, but the continuing unto the end yields the true glory. If we can thoroughly believe that this which we do is in defence of our religion and country no doubt our merciful God for His Christ our Saviour's sake is able and will

**Isaac Foot as Lord Mayor of Plymouth, 1945:** ▶
**'My grandfather was a true and proud son of Plymouth . . .'**

Upon this spot, on Sunday
December 7th, 1643, after hard fighting
for several hours, the Roundhead
Garrison of Plymouth made their
final rally, and routed the Cavalier
Army which had surprised the Outworks
and will night taken the town
For many years it was the custom to
celebrate the anniversary of this victory
long known as the 'Sabbath-day fight'
and counted as the 'Great Deliverance'
of the protracted siege,
successfully sustained by Towne and
Townsfolk on behalf of the Parliament
against the King under great hardships
for over four years.

give us victory, though our sins be red.'

He went on to proclaim, 'Drake took his drum with him all around the world. That is why its beat can be heard all round the world today. If you listen you can hear it — everywhere, in every land where Briton joins Briton to defeat this present menace of darkness and evil: in every distant station where two or three are gathered together in common danger and common hope. The young airman, high in the firmament, keeping guard over the Motherland, or striking day after day and night after night at the heart of the enemy's power — he can hear it: the sailor in whose veins Drake's blood still flows: the merchant seaman, who, even whilst I am speaking is risking his life to carry to and fro food and precious cargo. Everywhere throughout the whole Commonwealth the Drum can be heard.'

Five years later when he became Lord Mayor he had the broadcast printed and sent to all the schoolchildren of his beloved City, hoping they would keep alive the legend of Drake's drum which, as he said, 'can be heard everywhere where freedom is counted the precious thing'.

One of the things he was very happy to initiate while he was Lord Mayor of Plymouth was the commemoration of the raising of the siege of Plymouth in the Civil War 300 years previously. This epic period ended in the famous Sabbath Day Battle of Freedom Fields. The laying of the wreath on the Civil War Memorial at Freedom Park opposite his old home at Lipson Terrace became from then on an annual event. 'The Lord Mayor', the *Western Evening Herald* of 21 March 1946 reported — 'emphasises that the commemorations are in tribute alike to victor and vanquished in the memorable struggle which surged around the town and fortress.'

In 1960 when he was eighty years of age the then Lord Mayor of Plymouth, Mr Percy Washbourn, gave a large luncheon in his honour at the Grand Hotel in Plymouth. It was a chance for Plymouthians to pay their last respects to him. There were about 100 people present, amongst them eleven previous Lord Mayors of Plymouth, and five of his children.

Mr and Mrs Percy Washbourn remember the event vividly. My

◀Isaac laying a wreath on the Civil War Memorial to commemorate the raising of the siege of Plymouth.

grandfather was getting frail by then and had to remain seated most of the time, although he stood to make one of his last eloquent speeches. 'I remember him holding my hand tightly most of the time before and after the lunch', Mrs Washbourn told me.

His old friend Lord Birkett had been invited but was unable to attend though he sent the following message:

'I am delighted that Plymouth should so honour my old friend in this way, for he has always seemed to me to be that type of character of which the world stands so much in need, a man of strong opinions strongly held and fearlessly proclaimed in whose breast there has always been the love of liberty and the love of things which are honourable among men.

'He has been blessed with length of days and he has used the time for welfare of the community and it is a good thing to see him honoured in a City where he once occupied your high and honourable office.'

**The luncheon in Plymouth given by the Lord Mayor, Percy Washbourn, to mark Isaac's 80th birthday.**

Mr Washbourn, who had been my grandfather's friend on the Council of Plymouth for many years, told me that he had hoped to give my grandfather the Freedom of the City of Plymouth.

'If he had lived a few months longer', he told me, 'I think it would have come about.'

But in December of that year he died. However, although he would no doubt have gloried in that further honour the freedom of his beloved City, in his heart, was always his. For as a boy he had played in it and got to know it intimately, he had worked in and for the City and loved it all his life. In a way Plymouth intrinsically belonged to him as he belonged to it.

Recently I found an anonymous poem amongst his papers called *The Cromwell of His Day — a great Lord Mayor.* It was written at the end of his year of office — it ends:

*So we salute you Isaac, and we say*
*"Well done" and "thank you", not so much for what*
*You've done in these twelve arduous months, but more*
*For what you are, and what you've shown our schools*
*A Plymouth boy can be. We honour you,*
*And as long as Plymouth's records last, so long*
*Will this name, Isaac Foot, to us belong.*

# VII

# His End

*And death is a low mist which cannot blot
the brightness it may veil —*

*SHELLEY*

I was very sad not to be able to go to my grandfather's 80th birthday celebrations on 22 February 1960. There was a large family gathering at Pencrebar and he planted a tree with the help of his two great grandchildren Joanne and Andy Gordon — my cousin Kate's children — to commemorate the occasion.

He received hundreds of letters and telegrams from friends and relations all over the world. Amongst them many from his Liberal and Methodist associates in the Westcountry. Nancy Astor, Megan Lloyd George and his old friend Lord Birkett also sent their greetings. Lord Birkett kept to the old tradition of taking a quotation from the Bible for his missive — Psalm 91, Verse 16. My grandfather did not even have to look up his Bible to know it read:

'With long life will I satisfy him, and show him my salvation.'

The only one of his children not present on that occasion, the last of his birthdays, was my father. He was at that time Governor of Cyprus and nearing the end of his term there. Cyprus was shortly to gain her Independence and his telegram for the day read:

'So sorry we can't be with you tomorrow. We are confident we shall finish our job here soon and then we shall come to report to you. Pit and Rock — Love Mac.

My brother Paul wrote from Oxford where he was at University College and following in his uncle's footsteps was soon to become

◀Isaac Foot's 80th birthday: he plants
a tree with the help of his two great
grandchildren, Joanne and Andy Gordon.

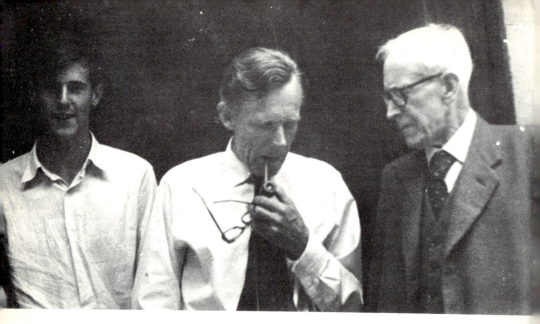

**Isaac Foot with son John and grandson Paul.**

President of the Union. His letter was in typical Foot tradition. It read:

*Dear Grandpa;*

> *Today is called the Feast of Isaac Foot,*
> *And future February's shall ne'er go by,*
> *But he in it shall be remembered.*

*Many Happy Returns of your birthday! 80 years of great achievement and learning are crowned today, and I hope the population of Callington (and I'll throw in Newbridge) will rise to the occasion with great rejoicing.*

*I am very excited at the moment as I go to America this week-end to debate for the Columbia Broadcasting Corporation! Quite something eh? I leave on Friday, and return on Monday. I think the motion will be for the abolition of capital punishment with reference to Chessman.*

*I am very busy and very happy, and look forward to seeing you and Kitty in March.*

*A saffron cake arrived yesterday and was devoured almost at once. Thank you. Pit and Rock. Many happy returns.*

> *Paul Mackintosh Foot*

Isaac's 80th birthday. Above: planting a tree.
Below: with two grandchildren and two great grandchildren.

So a third generation had inherited a love for literature and learning and oratory and saffron cake and a hatred for such inhumane practices as capital punishment. And a third generation was using my grandfather's family passwords — Pit and Rock.

But although my grandfather spoke out against capital punishment all his life and found the practice repugnant he characteristically had a funny story to relate on the subject.

A man called Jan was being led through the streets of his town to be hanged at a public execution. As he passed his house the window was thrown open and his wife leant out, 'Jan, where shall I plant the 'tatties?' she shouted as he passed below with his head bent. There came no answer. She shouted still louder, 'Jan, where shall I plant the 'tatties?' but there was still no answer. Once more Jan's wife called her question from the open window and when she still received no answer she slammed the window shut. 'Jan's vexed', she retorted, ''cause he's going to be hanged.'

*He was a man, take him for all in all,*
*I shall not look upon his like again.*

So said Hamlet of his father and it is what I feel so strongly about my grandfather. What sometimes hits me with surprising force is how much I think about him and his whole attitude to life, even now, twenty years after his death. In fact his influence seems to grow on me with every passing year.

I am often aware of doing things of which he would not approve but more than that I feel my pleasure in the things he would have enjoyed strengthened by what I know would have been his approval.

I have a portrait of him hanging in my drawing room. Sometimes when I am feeling agitated or cross or down-hearted the life-like painting of him seems to catch my eye. There is a half smile on his lips and an irresistable twinkle in his eye and I never fail to feel cheered. He seems to be saying, 'Nothing is that bad, look a bit further and you'll find something to laugh about.'

What never failed to amaze me was his broad scope of interests. I remember being home with my family from Jamaica when I was about thirteen years of age and we had taken a house for a few months in Surrey. He came to stay with us and was engrossed in the story of one of Sir Alfred Hitchcock's detective films he had just seen called *Dial M for Murder*. He was determined we should see it and gave us children the money for the cinema ticket so that we could go and see the film that had so caught his interest.

During another holiday I went to stay at Pencrebar for a few days. Grandpa and Kitty were driving up to London the following week and gave me a lift back. It was a perilous journey, his driving had become even more erratic over the years. He always assumed that near misses were the other driver's fault. 'Take that man's number' he would say to Kitty after each narrowly avoided collision. Kitty calmly took down the numbers, never commenting, realizing that any criticism of his driving would be useless and realizing that my grandfather would forget everything once the drive was over. Kitty and I often laughed about this habit of his. It seemed so strange, a man who never blamed another lightly for his actions was so completely unaware of being in the wrong behind the wheel of a car.

From the beginning of his driving life he and others were often in danger because of his driving. He seemed unable to concentrate on

**Receiving his honorary degree at Exeter University in 1959.**

the job, his mind always wandering to more interesting things. It was a miracle he never had a serious accident.

What amused me was to find out later that he had once been President of the Pedestrian Association, an organisation working nationally for the safety of those who were sometimes in peril because of their President's driving habits.

The last ten years of his life were still full of new and stimulating interests. In 1953 he was appointed Chairman of the Cornwall Quarter Sessions serving until 1955. And only a year before he died in 1959 he received another well deserved and greatly appreciated honour when he was given the honorary degree of D. Litt. by Exeter University.

In the last two years of his life I went fairly often to Pencrebar. He was growing thinner and weaker and yet to the last was full of fun. On one of these visits one of the girl friends with me had something lodged in her eye. We went to the doctor in Callington to

' . . . my father was back from Cyprus to enjoy his father's company during the last months.'

have it extracted. As we were leaving the doctor asked me to stay behind, 'How long will it be before your father is back from Cyprus?' he asked. 'Because I think he should know your grandfather is very ill, he has not long to go now.'

As I walked out into the sunny spring day I could not grasp the news. Stupidly I had never contemplated an end to his life.

I often wondered whether he suffered those last months. Although from photographs one can see he was fading away, when I was with him I hardly noticed. The hugeness of his inner vitality dispelled the horror of his physical decline.

Fortunately my father was back from Cyprus to enjoy his father's company during the last months. He and my mother were living nearby and spent a lot of time at Pencrebar. My father often speaks of the fact that he was still receiving valuable advice from his father about his future, even in these last few weeks.

These last years there were no longer any dogs at Pencrebar and all his affection for animals was lavished on a large, handsome tabby cat, called Oliver (after Cromwell, of course). He adored and spoilt the cat who was devoted to him and never far from his lap.

We still had happy gatherings over meals in the kitchen. After almost every meal he would push his chair back, slap his hands on his knees and say with great gusto, 'The Queen of England cannot have dined as well today.' Kitty beamed, always glad of the customary compliment and I felt a sense of reassurance — it was always good to hear the familiar phrases.

He was still reading, not only old favourites but new novels and biographies, sometimes drifting off to sleep with his book open on his lap. The pleasure he derived from music increased with the years. Johann Sebastian Bach's resonant chords boomed out over the house even more often than they had before.

In the end he seemed to die with the same grace that he had lived. He quite quietly faded away. My step-grandmother said she was woken in the night by the silence. She was so used to the sound of his breathing that when it stopped she woke with a start. He had gone. So on 13 December 1960 he died at his beloved Pencrebar in his own room looking out over the Lynher valley which he loved so much.

Most of the family gathered for the funeral. There was a Memorial Service in Plymouth and then the funeral service in Callington. He was buried at Callington cemetery.

**The Author with her husband and daughter at Pencrebar in 1962.**

When I arrived at Pencrebar on the day of his funeral Kitty met me at the door. 'Do you want to go up and see your grandfather?' she asked. For a moment I thought it had all been a mistake, he was still alive. But then I realised he had gone and the last thing I wanted to do was to see his body now. His liveliness, his grand emotions, his laughter, his quick jerky movements, his rich voice were what I wanted to remember.

When we watched his coffin go into the newly dug grave I did not feel at all that he was in that sombre box. His spirit was free and off on a new and exciting adventure. It was impossible to connect him in any way with death, but comforting to look up from his grave side and see his old loves Caradon Hill on one side and Kit Hill on the other. Back at Pencrebar the blow of his absence was softened by the presence of all the uncles and aunts and cousins there again. The books too were still there, the atmosphere was the one he had built up in that house over the years. It remained comforting to me.

A great friend of mine, Caren Meyer, who worked with me at that time on the *Evening News* in London wrote to me when my grandfather died:

*'I was quite shaken when I heard your grandfather had died. I know how fond you were of him. In a strange way I almost knew him, his wife and their home came so completely alive for me. It was your affection for him that brought him near, even for complete strangers.*

*This won't be much consolation for you, but to know that you obviously meant much to him, perhaps does.*

*Our favourite waitress enquired after you. 'Where is your friend?' she asked. 'I haven't seen her lately.' I told her that your grandfather had died. 'What a shame', she said, obviously sad about it. 'And just before Christmas too.'*

*At first I thought it queer to think of death in relation to Christmas. Then I pondered and perhaps it isn't strange after all.*

*I know how much you will miss him. Specially this Christmas. I read all the obits in the paper and he became to me even more remarkable than the man you had known and loved. Because until then I had not known all about his background. To me he was always a man of tremendous intellect and kindness who sat in a house in Cornwall, surrounded, no almost buried by books. Books, you told me, that he knew so well he could lay his hand on any volume at a moment's notice; books he'd tell you about and then suddenly fall asleep; and jokes he'd tell you, and electric blankets in the beds, waiting for you and Tim to arrive for the weekend.*

*I told you I knew him and it's you who made me know him. And in my clumsy stupid way I'm trying to say I share your sorrow.'*

It cheered me to think that I had communicated some of the greatness of his character to her, that yet another person, though a stranger to him, had fallen a little bit under his spell.

Kitty stayed on at Pencrebar for a few years. I still went when I could and when my daughter was born in June 1962 I took her. It was wonderful to look out of the front bedroom window down on the lawn and to see her sleeping there in her pram where I had slept at the same age. I felt happy that she too would be touched by the magic of Pencrebar.

The books had gone to America, the empty shelves were now covered by hessian, the house was lonelier and quieter but I still loved it.

Sometimes in the night I would wake and think I heard him shuffling through the passages grumbling at some light left turned on, or searching for a book on the landing. At other times running into the library I would be quite shocked not to find him sitting in his favourite chair deep in his reading. But when Pencrebar was sold he seemed to follow me everywhere.

Now that I live in Cornwall he becomes even closer. He is so connected with the places I love, the people I love, the things and ideas I love. It is his strong spirit that draws me back always to this part of the world, that makes it home for me.

# ACKNOWLEDGMENTS

When writing this book it was important to me to speak to as many Westcountry people as possible who could remember Isaac Foot and who had worked with him in politics, Methodism, literature or the law.

I am extremely grateful to all those who have given up their time to reminisce along with me. Each time I found it a most heart-warming experience.

My especial thanks must go to Stanley Goodman, my second cousin and a nephew of Isaac Foot, who read my manuscript and was able to tell me so much about my great grandparents, Isaac, the elder, and Eliza.

My uncles and my aunt Jennifer have also told me many stories I had either forgotten or which were new to me and what has never ceased to impress me is the really great love and respect all the children held for their parents.

Finally, my thanks go to Michael Williams. One sunny day we sat in a book shop in Lostwithiel and many of the people who came in that day, finding I was a granddaughter of Isaac Foot, were longing to speak to me about him and impart stories of him. I enjoyed talking to them all so much and when we left Michael turned to me and said, 'Why not write a book about your grandfather?' So it was entirely due to his idea and encouragement that this book has been written.

# ALSO AVAILABLE

## FOLLOWING THE TAMAR
by Sarah Foot. 55 photographs and map. Price £1.20.
Sarah Foot is the Tamar's inevitable author, living only a mile from its banks, seeing it every day from her Cornish home, and truly loving it.
'. . . both a labour of love and a work of subtle selection, combining the intriguing byways of local history and geography with a profusion of well-chosen black and white plates.'　　　　　　　　　Dick Benson-Gyles, The Western Evening Herald

## FOLLOWING THE RIVER FOWEY
by Sarah Foot. 49 photographs. Price £1.
Sarah Foot follows the Fowey from its beginnings on Bodmin Moor to where it meets the sea beyond Fowey and Polruan.
'She stitches into the simple tapestry of the river's story names and incidents and anecdotes, deftly and lovingly, every thread and every page touched with charm and an unashamed sense of delight.'　　　　　　　　　Western Morning News

## BODMIN MOOR
by E.V. Thompson. 45 photographs and map. Price £1.50.
E.V. Thompson, author of the bestselling novel, *Chase the Wind*, set on the eastern slopes of Bodmin Moor, explores the Moor past and present.
'. . . shows the moor in all its aspects — beautiful, harsh, romantic and almost cruel . . . how well he knows the character of the moor.'　　　The Editor, Cornish Guardian

## HAWKER COUNTRY
by Joan Rendell. 40 photographs, letters and map. Price £1.20.
Hawker Country is an area of North Cornwall, embracing some cruel, dramatic coastline and beautiful countryside: a corner of the Westcountry immortalised by the great Parson Hawker of Morwenstow.
'A book about that Prince of clerical eccentrics and the places associated with him . . . contains many pictures of great interest.'　　　　　　　The Church Times

**We shall be pleased to send you our catalogue giving full details of our growing list of titles for Devon and Cornwall and forthcoming publications.**

**If you have any difficulty in obtaining our titles, write direct to Bossiney Books, Lands End, St Teath, Bodmin, Cornwall. Books over 95p add 35p for postage and packing. Books under 95p add 30p for postage and packing.**